a.
C.
with love from Marie
+ Tyler

Marty on the Mountain

38 Years on Mount Washington

Martin Engstrom

Marty on the Mountain
38 Years on Mount Washington
By Martin Engstrom

Printed by:
Cardinal Printing Company
Route 117, P.O. Box 115
Denmark, Maine 04022

Published by:
Martin Engstrom
227 West Fryeburg Road
Fryeburg, Maine 04037

Printed In The United States of America.
Printed on acid free paper.

ISBN 0-9740967-0-9

Front Cover Photograph by Russ Heald

There is a new breed of mountain man, the men who stand their lonely watch atop the lonesome windswept mountain top, tending the big rigs, broadcasting television. For each engineer is a mountain man, equally familiar with multimeter and parka, waveform monitor and crampons, soldering gun and ice chisel, staking his life on his knowledge of both electric shock and frostbite, r.f. exposure limits and wind chill tables.

Thanks to my wife Rosalie who in some ways had as hard a job as I did, having to put up with me being gone for a week at a time, and to Dick Cushman, the best coworker and later the best boss anyone could have, and to my son Dan who was most helpful with the computer, and to Eunice Stone who did the first draft typing of some of the chapters, and to all the people of Channel Eight and its radio and microwave customers, and the people of the Observatory, State Park, Auto Road, Cog Railroad, and Appalachian Mountain Club. Many of whom have been friends through the good times and the bad times.

INTRODUCTION

At twenty seven years of age, fresh out of the U.S. Air Force, and with a brand new first class radio license, I got a job as a TV Engineer on Mount Washington at WMTW-TV 8. Little did I realize what adventures were in store for me in the next thirty eight years. The work shift was one week on, one week off, year round. That is, be at the Glen House base ready to go up at nine a.m. Wednesday morning, go up the eight mile long Auto Road by company truck in summer and by snow tractor in winter, relieve the other shift and stay until the other shift returned the next Wednesday. Once a day for thirty seconds Wednesday, Thursday, Friday, Monday, and Tuesday I would appear on camera during the news and weather. I would report the summit weather conditions as I saw them. From this I became known far and wide as the "Mount Washington Weather Man" which I most assuredly had no intention of doing. In this book I attempt to explain some of the other things that happened.

TABLE OF CONTENTS

A NEW JOB

February 10, 1964, there was a storm in the mountains that day, so I headed south instead of north in my quest for a job at a radio or TV station. After unsuccessfully applying at Channel 6 and Channel 13 in Portland, Maine, and one of the Portland radio stations, I marked out a route on a road map which would take me in a big circle to all the radio stations in the North Country. I knew very little about the broadcast industry, except that at an early age I became interested in electronics, and at that time being an Engineer at a radio station was about the ultimate job in electronics. But childhood dreams do not come that easy. Years ago, in 1956, when I left my home in the North Country to seek my fortune (as they say in the ancient fairy tales) I got a job as a Draftsman at Pratt & Whitney Aircraft in Connecticut. After three years, I had figured out that I didn't want to spend the rest of my life living in a city and working on paperwork in a big office building. The draft board was getting close to my age group, so I joined the U.S. Air Force. In basic training, the first letter that I got from home told me that my draft notice had arrived, so I timed that just about right. The Air Force put me through their longest and most technical tech school to work on the radar and computer weapons control systems in the F-101-B twin engine supersonic jet fighter plane, so I was into electronics in a big way at long last. After tech school, I took correspondence courses, and studied on my own until I was able to qualify for an FCC First Class Radiotelephone Operator License, the license that was required to work at a broadcast station. After getting discharged from the Air Force at the end of my hitch, I returned to my parents home in Fryeburg, Maine, to rest and collect my thoughts for about a month before settling down to some serious job hunting. There were more radio stations close together to the north, so I had intended to start out in that direction first, but with a snow storm in that direction I decided to go the other way around the route that I had marked out. The first point on my map was Poland Spring, home of the studio of WMTW-TV 8, Mount Washington TV. It was not difficult to find the Ricker Inn in the Poland Spring complex, then the offices of Channel 8. I asked the receptionist for a job application. After filling out the form, she asked me if I wanted to see the Chief Engineer. After an affirmative answer, she directed me to the engineering office, just across the hall from her desk. Chief Engineer, Parker Vincent introduced himself and directed me to a chair in his office. At this time Parker, as he wanted to be called, looked and talked exactly as Secretary of Defense, Casper Weinburger would appear on TV twenty years later. The office had floor to ceiling bookcases on two walls, and was cluttered with books, papers, maps, drawings, and electronic parts. Parker talked for nearly two hours, describing the mountains, Channel 8 and its problems in exacting detail. Then he said, "Well, what do you think?" I replied, "Sir, I perceive that you are trying to discourage me, but the more you say, the more interesting it sounds." He then said, "We may have an opening, I'll call you in a day or two." After discussing details of what I should bring, and where I should report if he did hire me, he said, "I wonder how that storm is doing on the mountain." He turned to the wall behind his desk to an old fashioned oak box magneto telephone with the dry cell batteries on the floor beneath it. There was a modern dial telephone on his desk. He spun the crank one long ring and picked up the handset. I asked, "Private line to the Mountain?" He replied, "It goes by a subcarrier on one of our microwave systems." That really struck me as odd, an antique crank telephone working through a microwave system. At that time microwave was as state of the art and high tech as satellite communications is now. Little did I realize how much of that sort of ancient and modern contrast I would soon encounter. Parker briefly discussed weather over the crank telephone, and told the person on the other end a little bit about me, then hung up. He promised to let me know one way or the other by tomorrow noon so that if he wanted me, I would have time to get some cold weather gear together to make the shift change trip Wednesday morning. This was on Monday. I left the office with my head spinning, and went straight home to await the 'phone call. The rest of that day, and all night and the next morning I thought of little else as I weighed the pros and cons, wondering if it was the right job for me, and hoping that it was. Shortly before noon, true to his word, Parker called and told me to be at the Glen House in Pinkham Notch at eight o'clock the next morning. Now to piece together an outfit. I had plenty of long underwear, warm shirts, and a second world war army parka, so I rushed over to North Conway to buy the heaviest wool hunting pants I could find and ski goggles and a face mask. Five buckle overshoes over work shoes always have been my preferred winter footgear. Parker had told me that the company provided food, bedding, towels, and tools, so all I had left to do was throw my shaver, toothbrush and some spare clothing into a zipper bag and my outfit was complete.

Wednesday morning I awoke early, and got dressed for an arctic climate. My mother prepared a good breakfast, and soon I was off for high adventure. The thirty five miles to the Glen House seemed like two hundred, but I arrived at about seven o'clock, and found no one else of the Mountain crew there. It was a beautiful crisp clear winter day, so the wait was quite pleasant except for wondering where everyone was. Later I found out that the official time to leave the base for the trip up has always been nine o'clock. Parker told me eight o'clock to be sure that I would be on time. Finally the rest of the TV crew arrived and introduce themselves. There was Phil Labbie, our driver, a French Canadian American from Berlin, tall, strong, and confidence inspiring. Lee Vincent, Transmitter Supervisor, Parker's son, and Willie Harris, a true gentleman of the old style, from Philadelphia, Pennsylvania, now from Jackson, New Hampshire. Also riding with us this day was Ed Breen, an FBI agent from the Boston office who had radio equipment in one of TV's buildings on the summit.

Phil unlocked and opened a garage door, and there

was our transportation which he began to check, as we loaded our baggage and groceries. The machine, a 1953 Tucker model 443 Sno-Cat, was a lot smaller than I had envisioned from the picture which Parker had shown me. It's cab, rather like a panel truck but smaller, set on four tracked pontoons. Tied onto the roof racks were sheets of plywood with lots of nails sticking through them. I was told that these were used for crossing glare ice. On the outside of the left side of the cab was a square metal box which housed a powerful gasoline burning heater to supplement the smaller gasoline heater in the drivers compartment. Ed got into the front seat with Phil. Lee, Willie and I piled into the back with our cargo and made ourselves as comfortable as possible on the bench seats which were along the sides. The rear compartment was separated from the driver's compartment by a huge gasoline tank with a wooden tool box on atop, leaving about a foot of space from the top of the tool box to the roof. As we crossed Route 16 between the Glen House and the Mount Washington Auto Road, remarks were made that crossing the busy highway was the most dangerous part of the whole trip.

Because it was such a clear beautiful day, we kept the back door open for ventilation and to admire the view. Despite it's awkward appearance, the old Sno-Cat rode quite smoothly as we ascended the road at a steady eight to ten miles per hour speed. For the first four miles below half way, the road was in trees with only occasional glimpses of distant valleys and mountains. Just after we passed the Half Way House and the four mile post, the machine tilted towards a deep ravine as we climbed over some deep drifted snow. Lee remarked, "This part of the road at 4000 feet elevation is called The Horn, and sometimes we have to shovel a path across it." After a few more sharp turns, and climbing over a few more drifts, we reached the five mile grade where we enjoyed a magnificent view of mountains and valleys to the east and south. As we made a sharp turn at Cragway Spring, I spotted a large building high above us. I asked Lee if that was the TV building, and he said, "No, that is the summit hotel, our buildings are on the other side of the summit, out of sight from here." Each turn of the road revealed greater and more magnificent views. As we continued to climb, the last of the trees were way below us, and there was no more vegetation visible through the snow. At Cragway Spring and about every half mile from there on was a twelve foot square boxlike building which Lee told me was a survival shelter. Soon we passed between two enormous metal buildings, the larger of which had a huge horn shaped duct sticking out one side. Lee told me that these were the Air Force icing research laboratory and dormitory. Then he pointed out five steel storage tanks each about ten feet in diameter and thirty feet long which is our winters supply of kerosene to run our diesel electric power plant. After another few hundred yards we climbed a steep, winding grade and arrived on level ground among buildings and towers. We parked close to a covered breezeway between a wood shingled two story building and a low flat roofed gray painted building. We climbed out of the machine and carried our luggage and supplies through the breezeway into the flat roofed building. Inside, after passing through a room crammed with racks and cabinets of electronic equipment, we found ourselves in a comfortable looking living quarters, where I was introduced to Norm Coulomb of Berlin, a former army Captain, now active in the National Guard, and Dave Berry, the man that I was hired to replace. Ed was given a key and went to another building to check his radios. Phil got a cup of coffee and a donut while Dave and Norm told Lee, Willie and I about the events of the previous week. After a while, Ed came back, returned the key, and got a cup of coffee. After a bit of light conversation, Phil, Ed, Dave and Norm went out to the Sno-Cat which had been running at a high idling speed, and headed down the Mountain.

With the shift change finished, Lee asked me if I had my license with me. The license is an impressive looking document eight by ten inches with scroll work edges suitable for framing. Mine was in a plastic page protector in my zipper bag. I got it out and Lee showed me where to hang it beside the others. I noted that I should get a good glass picture frame for it. I also noticed that mine was the only one with the Ship Radar endorsement. When I was in the Air Force, I had been proud to answer to the job title of "Radar," so I had gone to the effort of getting that extra credit on my license, although I have never needed it.

Lee showed me which bedroom, which bed and which dresser draws would be mine, then proceeded to show me around. The TV building is about thirty six feet wide by seventy six feet long, with the length of the building pointing about 330 degrees or about north west by north. This one building was to be most of my whole world for one week out of two for the next many years. The entrance door where we came in is at the north corner. The first twenty six feet at the north west end is the transmitter room, which contains the TV transmitter and it's associated equipment, our whole reason for being here. Near the center of the back wall of the transmitter room is a four foot wide French door into the living room which is thirteen feet wide in the center of the Building, and eighteen feet long. On one side are two bedrooms with two beds and two dressers in each. On the other side is a bathroom, kitchen and pantry. The kitchen has a window which faces 240 degrees or roughly southwest by west. This was one of those rare clear days when the view out this window included Whiteface Mountain in upstate New York, 131 miles away. The ten by fourteen foot pantry seemed to contain more food than the average neighborhood convenience store. Jammed into this small room were five deep freezers, one refrigerator, an electric clothes drier, and floor to ceiling shelves loaded with canned goods, household supplies and packaged foods. Enough to last a two man crew for a year. The groceries we brought up with us were only perishables such as milk, eggs and salad vegetables. Behind the living quarters is the switch room which contains the controls for the diesel electric power plant, the huge fuse boxes which distribute all the electric power for the whole summit, and a work bench which includes a drill press, a grinder, and all sorts of mechanical tools. Through another door, we entered the engine room. The noise level in this room made conversation impossible. A short flight of stairs led to the engine room floor about four feet below the floor in the rest of the building. In addition to fuel, lubricating oil and water tanks and a bank of batteries, there were three huge Caterpillar diesel engines hooked to generators. Two were 1662 cubic inch V-8's and one was a smaller four cylinder engine similar to the engine in a D-7 tractor. Beyond the engine room is a small, dirty, noisy, hot room cluttered with antennas, called the plenum chamber. The hot air from the engine radiator keeps ice from forming on the fiberglass wall in front of the antennas, before it is ducted outside through louver panels.

Back in the living quarters, as my ears stopped ringing from the roar of the engine room, Lee told me that WMTW-TV, the company we work for, also owns two other buildings on the summit which we have to take care of, but first it was time for lunch. It did not take long to put on the table a lunch of sandwiches and canned soup. As we ate, I noticed that Lee and Willie habitually glanced at the video monitors in the transmitter room frequently.

After lunch, Lee said, "while the weather is still good, I'll show you the other buildings." We put our coats and boots on and went outside. The small two floor building at the other end of the twenty foot long breezeway where we came in was the Weather Observatory. Lee showed me through TV's other buildings, the Yankee Building, and the Old Yankee Powerhouse, and pointed out two small wooden shacks about fifty feet down the side of the Mountain which contained a variety of antennas. After pointing out various antenna towers and microwave dish antennas, he pointed out Tip Top building on the highest point of the summit and just below it the summit hotel, now closed for the winter.

Back inside the TV building, the rest of the day was spent explaining what my duties would be and getting me settled into the living quarters.

FURTHER INTRODUCTION
TO THE SUMMIT

As we settled into the daily routine of summit life, I had a lot to learn in a hurry. Normally, there are two men on duty. One works the day shift which includes sign on, and the other works night shift which includes sign off. Because I was new and being trained, I was the third man on the shift, and would work both sign on and sign off, sleeping in between, to learn both ends of the job. The electronic training which I had received in the U.S. Air Force and the material which I studied to get my radio license gave me a good background in theory, but I knew just about nothing about the practical side of television broadcasting. Basically, a Transmitter Engineers job is to watch the equipment to be sure the picture and sound are going out all right, take meter readings periodically, do routine maintenance, and when something goes wrong, get service restored as soon as possible. The transmitter room looks frightfully complicated because everywhere you look there are dials, switches, meters, knobs, colored lights and picture monitors. Actually, looks are deceiving, the more complicated it looks, the easier it is to work with, because what we need to know is displayed somewhere. We don't have to waste a lot of time poking around with portable test instruments. At most transmitter sites, the programming arrives from the studio through a microwave receiver, then it is fed through the huge broadcast transmitter and out to the antenna. The Mount Washington site is much more complicated than that for two reasons. First, we are a relay site for a lot of different kinds of services, so there are a lot of signals going through here, and lots of different kinds of equipment. Second, there are no power lines within many miles of the summit, so we have to make our own electrical power with a diesel electric generating plant. Now in most places it is not too difficult to operate a quarter megawatt diesel plant, but on this Mountain there are extra problems. There is no practical way to haul diesel fuel up here in the winter, so we have to store a fantastic quantity. This gets us involved with tanks, valves, pumps, pipelines and all that sort of complications. Also, in order to make lots of electricity it is necessary to put a lot of cool air through the engine radiator. Most places that is not a big problem, but here the weather is so extreme and changes so fast, that we are constantly doing a balancing act between having an engine shut down on overheat, and filling the engine room full of snow and freezing up the water pipes. When a one hundred mph wind suddenly switches direction, some fast engine room acrobatics is called for.

The main thing which I had to do in this first week on the Mountain was to learn where each piece of equipment was, and what it did, and how everything is tied together through the switches and patch panels. In other words, I had to memorize a system block diagram which did not exist on paper. There was a four drawer file cabinet in the living quarters full of instruction manuals, but there was very little in it about how things were tied together. The other thing I had to learn was to recognize all the normal sounds in the building, and to react instantly to a sound which did not belong, or a minor defect in the picture. As is true in most TV stations, we do not usually keep the audio turned up unless we are working on a problem, or watching a program for our own entertainment. As a generality, it is bad business to have program audio of any kind on unnecessarily because it masks too other sounds, and unless the person on duty is closely following the plot of the program, he will not know which sounds to ignore and which to react to. Most defects in the audio won't be detectable unless it is turned up quite loud and the operator is concentrating on it, so as long as the meters on the console are bouncing around in a normal range, that is about all that can be done for routine monitoring. However, visitors do think it is strange that there are TV pictures everywhere they look, but no audio can be heard. Another thing which visitors notice is how the Engineers can be apparently completely relaxed, drinking coffee, reading or talking about unrelated things, then suddenly in reaction to something the visitor didn't even notice, jump up and rush to the transmitter room. Sometimes on a shift change, there could be all four operating Engineers and the Chief Engineer in the living room. It is an impressive scene to see five men suddenly move like greased lightning in response to an unseen signal.

Our whole reason for being here is to keep the television transmitter operating, everything else is on an "If you have some spare time" basis. However, a large portion of our concentration, worry, and mental energy is directed not at the TV transmitter, but at the engine room, because everything else is so totally dependent on it. The huge, slow turning Caterpillar diesels are designed for long life, and are probably the finest that money can buy. But one year of continuous running is about the same as driving a car or truck 200,000 miles. When I started on the Mountain the engines had been running for ten years, and they were not replaced until they were thirty years old. No matter how good an engine is, you have to expect that a few things will go wrong in six million miles of operation. One skill which I had to learn in this first week, was how to switch engines. What this means is that we start the other engine, adjust it to turn at exactly the same speed and in step with the one that is pulling the load, switch it's generator onto the line, get it to pick up the load as the other one releases it, trip that one off the line and shut it down, all without a trace of a flicker in the lights. Large commercial power plants routinely do this, but most small places running on homemade power such as camps, islands and sawmills don't even attempt it. They accept a second or so of lights off as they trip one engine off and then the other one on. When knowledgeable people are told about this, they usually tell horror stories of things they have seen or heard of, or had to straighten out the mess after someone else had fumbled a switch. Apparently, as I get the story, if the engines are not exactly in step when they are electrically switched together, spectacular things can happen, like snapped crankshafts, power units flipped upside down, engines torn loose from concrete bases, etc. Fortunately, we have never had anything like that happen here. But we always think about it just before we pull the lever.

There were many more things which I had to learn this first week on the Mountain. It seemed like only two or three days had gone by when suddenly it was Wednesday again and time for the shift change. Somewhere in the past few days, Lee had explained to me that the plan was that Willie was staying up another week and would be on shift with Norm Coulomb to replace Dave Berry who was now gone. Sometime later I would have to work two weeks in a row, and Willie would have two weeks off to switch us so that I would work with Norm, and Willie with lee. About 10:00 a.m. Phil and Norm arrived, and soon Lee and I were on the way down the Mountain.

THE WEATHER SHOW

Late in the afternoon of my first day on the Mountain, Transmitter Supervisor, Lee Vincent told me, "You are going on camera to do a live weather show. Start thinking what you are going to say." Now that came as a complete surprise. I don't remember that Parker Vincent told me anything about a live weather show from the Mountain in the two hours that he talked to me before he hired me. At home we didn't usually watch Channel 8 news because it didn't come in very well, because of a ridge of hills in the way. If I had ever seen the Channel 8 news and weather, it never occurred to me that part of it was live from the transmitter site on Mount Washington. Lee said, "Don't worry about it, I'll help you. First, I'll show you how to set up the camera." From one corner of the living room he got a rickety wooden tripod which was in two parts. The first part was three thin boards held together at one end by a loose bolt. He laid this on the floor and kicked the boards to point in three directions. The tripod itself had no stops to prevent the legs from spreading. Each leg had a nail sticking out of the end which fitted into a hole in the end of each of the three boards. I don't remember anything about the tilt and pan head, but it must have had one. At it's best, the whole thing was sort of floppy. The camera was out in the transmitter room. It was a vidicon unit, not the kind of camera that would normally be used in a TV studio. The camera head was a gray steel box about four by six by twelve inches with a big cable attached to one end and a home movie camera lens attached to the other end. It was set on a homemade steel frame looking into a slide projector which contained various test pattern and trouble slides. About fifty feet of cable was coiled up and hung on a spike in the wall beneath the slide projector frame. Lee slid the camera back out of the grooves it set in, and explained to me that it should always be carried with the lens pointing up to prevent any loose particles inside the camera tube from getting on the inside of the light sensitive front of the tube. He carefully mounted the head on the shaky tripod, and pointed it at a small steel desk in the back of the room. The rest of the camera filled one whole seven foot rack in the transmitter room, and there was a control panel in the transmitter control console. When the switch was turned on to warm it up, the vacuum tubes flashed and flickered for a while then settled down to a steady glow. While the camera warmed up, Lee showed me how to gather information and write a script. Years ago, when the station first started, the crew at the weather observatory next door did the weather show. First, audio only with a slide of some mountain scene, then later, on camera as we were about to do it. As I get the story, they showed the bad judgment of asking for more money when our company was thinking of asking them if they would do it for less. The decision was made that the transmitter engineers would do the show themselves. The Observatory would not give us the information free after they had been getting paid for it, so Channel 8 bought their own weather instruments so we could gather our own information.

　With the script written, we went through a very elaborate procedure of adjusting the camera. It required a lot of light, so there were six 300 watt photo flood lights hung from the ceiling. Lee coached me on how to act on camera, and told me to smile at the end. I forced an enormous smile which became my trade mark over the years. As the time approached, Lee sat at the console to switch me on and off at the appropriate time, then we had to shut the camera off and put it away. Because the process of setting up the camera and getting ready was so elaborate, I never did have a problem with stage fright.

Over the years the Mountain weather show always did require a disproportionate amount of time and effort. One day someone from the studio watched us setting up the camera, and remarked, "At the studio we do a half hour of news, sports, and weather with less fuss than this." For a good many years, we did two shows a day. In the 6:00 p.m. news the night shift man would sit at the console and switch, but in the 11:00 p.m. news, the day shift man was usually sleeping, so we had a switch on a long length of zip cord which allowed the night shift man to switch himself in front of the camera. I don't remember that it ever happened, but there was always speculation about what to do if the Engineer alone on duty was on camera and couldn't switch back to the studio. Obviously, he would have to get up and walk off camera to switch out in the transmitter room. The transmitter master switching system was homemade and crude. It involved among other things handmade control and relay boxes and parts of an Identification Friend or Foe system out of a second world war bomber. Two switches had to be moved in the correct order and a patch cord for the audio had to be put in to prepare for the weather show switch, then returned to normal afterward. Wrong moves would result in loss of picture and/or sound or failure to switch. At it's best, all home receivers would roll their picture vertically momentarily when the switch was done. Sometimes our local sync generator would be far enough off frequency that that some home receivers could not make a steady picture at all during our weather show. So far as we know, the 11:00 p.m. weather show was the only completely one man show in commercial broadcasting. Where one man operates the equipment, including the generating plant which powers it, sets up the camera, gathers the information, writes the script, switches himself and does the show.

The most critical part of the camera is the vidicon tube. The one in the camera, and all of our spares were rejects from the studio. Many years after all other programming was in color we still did our Mountain weather show in weak, noisy black and white. Eventually we did get a different tripod. It had been a very high quality one, but when we got it, the legs would not fold, the elevator crank was broken off. And the camera mount stud had been lost and replaced with a stove bolt, but it was a gigantic improvement. A few months before the Mountain weather show was eliminated for eleven years, we got rid of all that junk and got an early model portable color camera. It required a lot of light to make a picture, and it was difficult to color balance the old fashioned photoflood lamps we were using, but the new camera did have a zoom lens, a view finder, and a good tripod. We got the new camera because the news department had gotten better ones and didn't want that one around. But for us it was a tremendous leap into modern times.

Audio always was a problem. Broadcast studios normally are kept quiet, and broadcast microphones are designed to be used well away from the person talking. In our living room where we did the weather show, there is always a high level of hum and rumble from the transmitters in one end of the building, and the diesel generators in the other end. We don't even hear it as long as things are running normally, but it was quite noticeable to the home viewers. Originally we used an old RCA desk mike which we set on a tall coffee can to get it closer to the persons mouth. It looked crude and sounded worse, but then, what didn't in this show. One Fourth of July, as a joke I laid a firecracker on top of the mike and taped it in place. When Transmitter Supervisor, Lee, saw it, he thought that it was such a good idea that he lit the fuse. That was the end of that mike. The studio sent us a lavaliere mike to use. That kind of mike hangs on a string around a persons neck, but that picked up too much room noise, so I made a stand for it out of welding rod. It worked quite well that way, but it looked bad enough to shame someone at the studio into sending us a modern microphone with a tall flexible stand. We could get that one close to our mouths and it was made to sound good that way.

A typical weather show would go like this. For example, say Ray Mercier was doing the studio weather show, and I was doing the Mountain show. After part of the studio weather, there would be a commercial, then back to Ray. He would say something like, "Marty Engstrom is on the Mountain tonight. Is it still clear up there Marty?" We would switch, and I would say, "Thank you Ray and good evening. This has been a truly magnificent day with 130 miles visibility all day climaxed by a rose, crimson, gold and violet sunset. Now the wind is from the north west at 55 miles per hour, the temperature is 12 degrees below zero, making the wind chill about 75 below, barometric pressure is 23.60 and rising. And now back to Ray Mercier." Then we would switch back and Ray would finish the show. Our part was only thirty seconds long, but it is surprising how much can be done in thirty seconds if it is planned carefully. We did all sorts of things to make the show interesting, such as showing pieces of rime ice, or pieces of equipment. When we got the color camera, sometimes we would point it out the kitchen window for a particularly colorful sunset. Once I wore our industrial hard hat as I described ice falling off the towers onto the roof of our building. Sometimes when it was extra cold, Willie would wear his parka and other cold weather gear. Once when we had a lot of ice on the ground, I showed a boot with a crampon attached. That was with the black and white camera. The nickel plated points sparkled and glittered in the light and looked at least twice size. I don't remember if we ever actually did it, but we often talked about throwing darts at a dart board on camera, and explaining that that is where we got our weather information. Actually, we had a good barograph in the living quarters, there was a home type thermometer out in the breezeway, and we had a hand held wind speed indicator. We made no attempt at measuring precipitation, and everything else was just look and guess.

It is important to understand, that those of us who did the Mountain weather show over the years were all TV engineers. None of us had any intention of being weathermen, actors, or TV announcers. Some people did it grudgingly, some people made sure that everyone around them and the viewers knew how much they disliked it. Personally, as a Maine

Backwoodsman, I have always taken the attitude that anything that needed to be done, and anything that I was asked or told to do, I could and would do it, and do a good job of it. Over the years, this attitude has led me into some strange adventures, but concerning the weather show it worked out well for me. I always put on a dress shirt and necktie, frequently a cowboy type bow tie which together with my smile became my trademark throughout the North Country. Partly or mostly because of being known through the weather show, I was able to put together a slide show which has taken me many places, but that's another story.

In the late 1970's and early 1980's we did all sorts of work changing equipment around, replacing FM and TV transmitters and such. The late weather show was canceled because we had equipment temporally in the way which made the one man show awkward to do. (An excuse, not really a reason.) Many times we were so busy with technical work that we didn't have time for the show and had to cancel it. This reason was real most of the time. Finally, on July 27, 1981, we were told, "until further notice, no more weather shows." We heard rumors that management thought that our show just didn't look professional enough. It just didn't fit in with the station image that they were trying for. Admittedly, in a well run station you seldom see a house cat walk across the desk in front of the person trying to do a show, but that was the sort of thing that made our viewers tune in to our station instead of some other.

In 1992, 11 years later, the decision was made to reinstate the weather show, but now I would be the only person doing it. No use making people do it who made it a point to show how much they disliked it.

The studio sent us another camera, one the news department had discarded, but still an improvement. This one needed only two 150 watt photoflood lights, so that made things a lot easier. We bolted a swing arm computer monitor mount to the wall and mounted the camera on it so it would fold flat against the wall when not in use. We made arrangements to hang a backdrop picture in a doorway and wired in connections for the microphone and I.F.B. I.F.B. is the ear piece that you sometimes see news people wearing, it carries program audio interrupted by the director's commands and comments. After a few months and a lot of comments by news directors and others, the studio sent us an up to date microphone. Then we had an almost good set up, and that is the way we continued until the very end.

PUSHKA

September 5, 1970, next door at the observatory D.F.C. the cat had just had kittens. The date has always been easy for me to remember because my daughter, Anita was born the same day. Transmitter Supervisor, Lee Vincent, asked us all if we would like to have a cat in the station. We all agreed that we would, so Lee asked for and got the pick of the litter. A few weeks later, when the kittens were old enough to leave their mother, Lee chose what appeared to be the most active one, a male orange and yellow tiger with large white patches. There was quite a bit of discussion concerning how a sensitive animal like a cat would react in the busy environment of the TV station, with the steady hum and rumble of machinery, and people coming and going. I suppose we needn't have worried, cats are very adaptable, and get along well in all sorts of noisy and active environments such as farms, factories and ships. The new kitten eagerly explored it's new home, and a problem we hadn't considered soon became apparent. We have quite a problem with soot. Freshly painted walls and ceilings soon look dingy, video monitors have to be cleaned weekly, and the big transmitters require constant attention or their insides soon look like they had been exposed to a smoky fire. We are not sure how much of it is from our diesels, and how much is from the Cog Railroad, but we believe that the high voltage in the transmitters attracts it. Cats are noted for keeping themselves clean, but our new kitten was overwhelmed by our variety of soot, and soon looked like he had been dragged through a coal bin. Until he was full grown, we found in necessary about once a week to put him in the kitchen sink and rub water into his fur until he howled with indignation, then we would provide a warm area for him to stay in until he dried out. Even in old age, his white areas were usually dull gray.

Pushka's mother, D.F.C., was a three colored cat which Greg Gordon, one of the observers brought up the Mountain as a kitten several years earlier. He brought her up in the winter time in a cardboard box in our old Tucker Sno-Cat. Her name D.F.C., stands for "Darn Fool Cat," or something like that. The one thing about observatory life that D.F.C. was really unhappy about was that there were no male cats around. It came as quite a surprise to everyone when she did become pregnant. We wondered if she may have mated with a bobcat, or if she had gone to the base of the Mountain, or if some cat in the valley had walked up. The most likely possibility was that one of the workers in the Summit House had a large altered male cat which we suspect may not have been as altered as his owner thought he was.

After our new kitten had wandered through our TV weather show a few times, it was decided to have a "Name the Cat" contest. Hundreds of letters and post cards poured in from all over the North Country. We selected the winning entry, "Pushka," which we were told was the Eskimo word for "cat."

Pushka soon grew into a handsome young cat. We fed him almost exclusively the best canned tuna fish cat food, which he earned with his frequent appearances on our TV weather show, where he probably did more than anyone else ever did to get people to watch Channel 8 news. Many people like cats, but they are seldom seen on TV because they are just too independent to be trained to follow any kind of script. Therefore, most TV directors putting together a carefully planned show are reluctant to include an unpredictable element such as a cat. Our half minute long live insert into the studios weather show was admittedly rather crude. Among other things, it was done with a worn out black and white camera long after everything else was in color. So if Pushka chose to walk across the desk and rub against the microphone causing the person doing the show to peer around him and grab the mike and push him off the script, it didn't hurt a bit, it added a nice homey touch which the viewers really enjoyed. If, however, Pushka wasn't around at the time, or just didn't feel like going on camera, that didn't hurt the show too badly either. The few times we wrote a script to specifically include him, things generally went rather badly. Once when I really wanted him included I tried to hold him until we went on the air. At just about the time we switched on, he was getting mad. He no longer was trying to get away, but was starting to bite and claw. All I could do was read the script, keep smiling and hope that no one got the wrong idea and called the animal humane society. In later years, I found it helpful to keep a few crumbs of catnip in the pocket of the shirt that I wore on the weather show. We had to be careful not to give him too much catnip however, because he really did get high on it.

Much of the fan mail we received over the years was either addressed to Pushka or mentioned him, and as I travel around the North Country doing my slide show about the Mountain, people frequently inquire about him. One thing that people are always surprised to hear is that Pushka and the observatory cats do go outside in the bad winter weather. Sometimes they don't stay outside very long, however. Cats are built low to the ground, and as clever hunters they are smart about taking advantage of the natural cover, so they don't get the full force of the wind. Also, as hunters they are familiar with all sorts of small openings which they can crawl into for shelter. They can always get into the engine room through the ventilation louvers and then into the cellar of the TV building, but considering the noise level, this has to be a last ditch emergency procedure. Once, during a bad storm, Pushka hadn't been seen for about three days, and we were sure he had perished. In the middle of the night I woke up to hear meow, meow, meow, meow! I got up, turned on the light, and out from under the bed he came. He was warm and dry, so I pushed him out into the living room where I knew Willie would feed him. The next morning , the question was, "How did he get into my room?" We found that under the bed was a hole in the wooden floor which no one knew about because it was covered with a loose floor tile which he had simply pushed aside to come up from the cellar. This was also the first time we knew that he would come in through the engine room despite the noise. There is no telling how long he had been in the cellar warm and dry while we were worrying about him.

One cat story involves Pushka's mother, D.F.C. The entrance to the old observatory was about eight feet above ground level with a stairway leading up to it. The wind is usually from the north west and would blow from the left as anyone went out this door, so over the years D.F.C. had learned to brace herself to be hit with wind from the left as she went outside.

One day the wind was from the south at about eighty mph, and so it was blowing from the right across the stairs. D.F.C. braced to the left as she always did and stepped outside, swish! Splat! She landed out in the rocks with a startled look on her face. Nothing was hurt but her dignity, but the story has stood as a standard for anyone who gets hit with a problem which is the opposite of what they were expecting.

When Pushka as a kitten started exploring the TV station, we were concerned about him crawling around inside the racks of equipment, because we knew that some of them contained exposed terminal strips with several hundred volts of electricity on them. Chief Engineer, Parker Vincent, said "Don't worry about it, cats know all about electricity, they invented it." Pushka never developed a fear of crawling through the racks, so he must never have gotten a real jolt from any of the exposed voltages. Of course, this is typical of cats. All they ask is a little food and water and a warm place to sleep, beyond that they take care of themselves and solve their own problems.

We always worried that some tourist would pick him up and take him home thinking that he was a stray in need of help, but this never happened, probably because he was always very cautious around strangers. Even inside our building, when anyone came in other than regular Mountain crew, he would run and hide. He was better than a watch dog. He would be sound asleep, then he would waken, crouch low to the floor and slink off to hide. We knew that he had heard the outer door open and close, and soon someone would come through the transmitter room to see us. Sometimes I worked this against him. He would be sleeping in the chair that I wanted to sit in, so instead of picking him up and setting him elsewhere, I would quietly walk out to the door, open and close it, and come back. He would be nowhere in sight, and would not be seen again for a half hour or so.

One pleasant summer day my wife drove up the Mountain with our children, Ralph, age four, and Anita, age three. She brought the children into the living room, then she and I went out to her vehicle to carry in some things. Pushka came in and strolled slowly through the transmitter room, relaxed, unconcerned. After all, he was in his home, why should he worry? He came around the corner to the living room door, and came face to face with Ralph, who said, "Kitty, kitty!" Pushka turned to run, but I was standing right behind him. I caught him and tossed him into the living room with the children, and shut the door. I went to help my wife carry in some more things, and when I returned the children were looking under my bed where Pushka was hiding. After they were properly introduced, he relaxed a bit and we opened the door so he could hide in the transmitter room when he didn't want to be sociable.

Another of Pushka's dislikes was dogs. Parker had a tiny red long hair Chihuahua, named Sherlock, which probably weighed less than half what Pushka weighed, yet Pushka was never comfortable when Sherlok was around and usually made it a point to be somewhere else until Sherlock left. One of our radio customers had an Irish setter which he frequently brought with him. One day we watched an interesting psychological byplay between Pushka and the radio customer's dog. The dog wanted to chase the cat, but knew that it would not be any fun unless the cat was afraid of him and tried to run away. Pushka wanted to go someplace and hide but he knew better than to run because then the dog would be right behind him, so he tried to act bored and unconcerned. He would try to look like he was thinking, "Well, nothing of interest here, may as well leave." Then he would start to stroll towards the door without looking at the dog. The dog wasn't buying the act, however. Every time the cat started towards the door, the dog would perk up and look like he was thinking, "We may get some action here yet." Finally Pushka made a break for it and made it to one of his hiding places, and the dog laid down again and looked disappointed.

It is truly amazing how many small rodents such as flying squirrels, mice and voles a well fed house cat can catch. One day we moved a parts cabinet and back of it we found Pushka's "trophy room," a big pile of feathers, squirrel tails and other yuckey things better left unmentioned. At one point a visiting biology student expressed concern that Pushka and the observatory cats might be endangering some rare species of these little creatures. One small rodent which is quite plentiful here, but some people have never seen, is flying squirrels. They don't really fly, they just glide after jumping off high spots. They are very light and fluffy with web membranes between their front and hind legs. These were always a major supplement to Pushka's diet. One day I looked out the window just in time to see a big gray squirrel go by with Pushka in hot pursuit. Back and forth and around and around they went, but this time Pushka went hungry, because squirrels are better than cats at climbing metal towers.

The most amazing thing is that Pushka killed at least four weasels that we know of. These are vicious little critters and it is generally believed that cats do not survive in a confrontation with one. Once in the

29

summer Pushka came in and presented me with a mouse. The mouse was still alive, so I threw it out the window. Pushka went out after it, so I closed the window. About half an hour later I believed that the matter had probably been settled, so I opened the window. Five minutes later Pushka strolled in his usual unexcited manner, and went to his water dish for a drink. I picked him up to pet him and noticed a strong strange smell which I didn't immediately recognize. About then Willie hollered from the transmitter room, "come look at this!" There on the floor lay a dead weasel, still warm, with a big blood stain under it's throat and no other marks of violence, and not a mark on Pushka, just that odd smell which I now recognized as the scent of the weasel. Pushka may have looked slow and lazy at times, but when there was game to be hunted, he was quick as a flash. But after nearly fifteen years, which is a ripe old age for a cat, he died on August 29, 1985, and we buried him in a deep hole in the rocks of the Mountain which was his home.

PARKER VINCENT

The major central character in the story of Mount Washington TV is Parker Vincent. Anyone who knew him can tell stories about him all day long. He was Chief Engineer from the beginning until he retired about 1985. In the early days of TV broadcasting he built the station and made it a success when everyone who knew anything about it said that it couldn't be done. That is what he should be primarily remembered for. He was a very strong personality resembling Mr. Dithers of the Dagwood and Blondie comic strip. He looked and talked just like Casper Weinburger who was Secretary of Defense under President Reagan. When explaining complex subjects to anyone he had a very condescending and helpful tone of voice that seemed to say, "The reason you don't understand this is that you are not as smart as I am, that's ok, nobody is." His rule was always, he was right, everyone else was wrong. It didn't matter what the station manager or the station owners wanted, it didn't matter what local, state, or federal laws or FCC rules required, it didn't matter what the laws of physics dictated, things would be done Parkers way, that was it, no room for argument or discussion. I have seen him take a half hour to convince an FCC inspector of something that was physically impossible. He had the most incredible luck, I have often said that if you were caught out in an open field during a thunderstorm you would do well to stand close to Parker. Lightning would never dare to hit him, he simply would not allow it. That is close to a direct quote by the way. Once as he was bypassing the safety interlocks on a high voltage cabinet of a big transmitter he remarked, "I will not be defeated by control system problems, I simply will not allow it."

When Parker drove a car, truck or snow tractor, his driving style resembled the cartoon character Mr. Magoo. As he blindly charged ahead at full throttle with his passengers fearing for their lives he would say, "Now now boys don't worry about a thing, I am an expert at this, I have been doing it for years." He could pass a whole line of cars around a curve or over a hill and there just would not be anyone in the oncoming lane when he did it. Out on the highway when he saw a big truck ahead he would speed up to catch and pass it while saying, "what's that truck doing on the road, they shouldn't allow rigs like that on this road. Doesn't he know that I have to get to Boston to fix the microwave?" As though the whole world revolved around Parker and his problems.

Two stories about Parker's luck. Once upon a time he and the crew were heading somewhere to work on a microwave link. They stopped for gas and Phil Labbie pointed out, "You've got a soft tire on your car." Parker answered, "Yes, I've had to keep adding air to that, I'll fix that." He drove over to the air hose and held the hose on, and held it on, and held it on, and held it on. He probably put full tank pressure in the tire. If you or I or anyone else did a stunt like that it would probably blow up in their face and kill them, but not Parker. The tire waited until everyone was safely in the office paying for the gas, then KA-BLAM! As loud as a big truck tire the whole side blew out. Phil said, "Well I guess that settles that." Parker said, "Yes I guess it does. I'll put the spare on and catch up to you at the microwave site."

The other story. Years ago Parker had a really nice twin engine boat. He had some work done on it in the winter. In the spring he set out to drive it across the bay to where he kept it for the summer. He began to smell gasoline. The smell got stronger, then one engine quit. He thought, "Well, I'll have to check that when I get anchored." To make a long story short, it turned out that the place that serviced the boat had filled the drinking water tank with gasoline. The hot water for the galley and head was heated by a heat exchanger on the exhaust manifold of one engine. That was the engine that quit for a totally unrelated reason. If it hadn't quit when it did, the boat with Parker in it would have exploded out in the middle of Casco Bay and no one would have ever known why. The crowning insult came when the boat repair place insisted that he pay for the gasoline that they put in the drinking water tank. That led to quite a law suite.

Here is an example of how Parker could get around FCC regulations. When the station was built, we needed to carry ABC network programming. The feed was available in Boston, but how to get it to the Mountain was the problem. In those days there was no way to license a TV intercity relay microwave except as a common carrier, and that meant that only the telephone company could do it, and that was expensive. We could license an STL (Studio to Transmitter Link) however. Now if we had a studio in Boston….. Parker always bragged that Boston was his town, he knew everyone who was important there. He talked to his friend the Monsignor of the Roman Catholic Church. Note: Parker wasn't Roman Catholic, he was Episcopalian. They worked out a deal. The church would give us a room which we could call a remote studio, and we would broadcast their Mass every Sunday morning. Now that we had a "studio" in Boston it was easy to license an STL. Five hops of vacuum tube equipment which was none too reliable in those days. A chain is only as strong as it's weakest link and when it quits working, guess which hop is in trouble and where to send the troops to repair it. But it worked and worked quite well for many years, mostly on Parker's stubbornness.

One person who knew Parker quite well explained to me, "Parker is primarily an Engineer but his biggest talent is his ability to get things past the FCC that no one else can." From what I have seen I am inclined to agree. The Boston microwave was just one of many deals which he was able to do. Another person told me that at any other station he wanted to do business with, he would talk to the station manager, not the Chief Engineer, but at Channel 8 Parker was the whole deal.

Here is an example of the sort of technical stuff that Parker could do that no one else would even attempt. In the 1960s TV remote production was a real big deal requiring a large truck or bus type of van and tons of equipment. The state of electronic news gathering as we now know it was many years away. Field work, if it wasn't live on air was all done with film cameras. The decision was made to carry live ball games from Boston. Anyone else would have said, "We can't do that, we don't have the equipment, and it would cost a small fortune to buy or rent it." But that wasn't Parker's style. In those days a TV camera was so big and heavy that it required two men to lift it onto its mount, and that was just the pick up head, most of the camera was rack mounted equipment. The station had an RCA field camera which was mostly the same as studio equipment except that the rack mount parts were in transport cases, and it had a very strong tripod instead of a wheeled dolly. This was as portable as you could get but it was most of a load for a pickup truck. Zoom lenses were rare and expensive. There was one on one of the two studio cameras. Parker borrowed that for the field camera, and loaded the whole thing into the station's 1955 Chevrolet half ton panel truck together with an old fashioned portable audio box, a few microphones, lots of cables, and one end of a hop of microwave to get the signal into our Boston microwave system. Dick Cushman tells of pulling up to the stadium gate with the radiator boiling, the clutch smoking and the blue and white paint job faded from sitting outside for ten years. The gate guard said, "You can park that over there. when your van gets here, send it in." Dick had to tell him, "This is it, this is our whole operation." Although it is ridiculous to try, it is just barely possible to do a whole ball game with just one camera and a zoom lens, we did it and it worked all right. Instant replay was something that only the big boys did and it was considered to be out of reach for a little back woods station like Channel 8, but we did it anyway. At the studio we had only two video tape machines. One was used for all the breaks and commercials. The other one continuously recorded the program coming in on the microwave which was also going into the transmitter on the air live. When the announcer on the field would say, "Lets see an instant replay on that last play," the studio crew would hit "rewind", then "play" and switch it on air. When it reached the end of what was recorded, they would switch back to the live feed. The announcer was watching the whole thing on an ordinary TV set tuned to the station so he knew when

35

to say what. The whole thing worked a lot smoother than it sounds like it should have. But with Parker style engineering, that's the way things usually worked.

But not always. One day Parker rigged up a complicated test set up which included a microwave power supply. After quite a few minutes of, "This goes here and this wire goes here," Parker plugged the power supply into a wall outlet. BANG! About as loud as a .38 revolver. We all stood there in shock for a few seconds, then Phil said, "Well I guess that settles that." Parker said, "Yes I guess it does." Then I noticed something we had all overlooked. I pointed to the nameplate on the power supply where it was marked "input 28 volts D.C." Parker had plugged it into the standard 120 volt A.C. wall outlet. Parker exclaimed sadly, " Ok, that explains it. Lets take the cover off and find out what happened." With the cover removed it was obvious. An electrolytic capacitor had blown. The capacitor was about an inch in diameter and about two inches long with wire leads coming out each end. The leads were bent down and soldered to the circuit board. The capacitor had ceased to exist, it must have vaporized. There were no bits of metal or paper laying around, not even a streak of soot on the circuit board. Just the two wire leads standing up from the board with the ends bent at right angles pointing at each other.

In 1981 we got a new TV transmitter. An RCA TTG-17H, the first one of its model shipped from the factory. It was delivered near the end of winter and had to be stored in the Glen House garage until the road was opened to wheeled vehicles in the spring. The major parts were three cabinets, each about twice as big as a home refrigerator, and the diplexer which combines visual and aural outputs. In its crate the diplexer was about the size and weight of an upright piano. The first wheeled vehicle up the road that year was our truck with the diplexer on a snow machine trailer behind. A snow tractor was in front in case it was needed to pull, and another was behind in case it was needed to push. When they arrived on the summit Phil reported, "All the way Parker was yelling take it easy, take it easy, and I just kept going."

Later, when we were ready to move the cabinets into the building, Joe Novic, Company Photographer, got me aside and asked, "What's the matter with Parker, can't he see that those things are two inches wider than the door way he wants to bring them in through?" I replied, "Don't worry about it, Parker is a determined man, he is determined that he will bring those cabinets in through that door way, and he will do it. Just watch and learn." We took the cabinet doors off, and we took the building door casing apart back to the studs. There was space enough for the cabinets to come through with the thickness of a sheet of paper to spare. Then they were too tall by an inch to go under a sheet metal cooling air duct. Parker ranted and raved, " they don't meet specs, according to the installation drawing they should fit." A few minutes work with a big hammer bashed the duct up enough to solve that problem. The rest of the installation was fairly routine, or at least as routine as anything could be with Parker involved. The factory had stipulated, "Do not fire it up until the factory tech. reps. get there." That is the kind of instruction that Parker would never heed, so of course as soon as the assembly was complete we started the initial start up and check out. When we got to the point of "High Voltage On," the rigs main circuit breaker instantly tripped. We found that the output lead from the high voltage power supply was connected solidly to ground. A mistake? We don't think so. We think that the factory crew did it intentionally because they knew what Parker would do. Anyway, it was easy enough to hook the lead where it belonged and complete the rest of the check out procedure. Anyway when the factory tech. rep. arrived he wasn't too surprised to find that the check out was completed and the rig was up and running.

PLOWING THE ROAD

One day in April dawned clear and mild. We could see that the snow in the valley was getting thin, but on the summit, winter had not yet started to loosen it's grip. Around 11:00 a.m. Phil Labbie arrived on the summit with the old Tucker Sno-Cat. He said that he had come up the cut off trail as we had been doing all winter, and now it was time to try to open up five mile grade. He would do this with another machine, and he wanted one of us to come with him in the Tucker in case he got stuck. Norm and I discussed what was involved, and it was decided that I would go and help Phil. We ate a quick lunch, then Phil got the other machine out of a small garage in the end of Yankee building. The other machine was a Bombardier Muskeg Tractor, made by the same company that first developed the small one and two man open cockpit snow sleds that are so popular now. The Muskeg Tractor was apparently designed for hauling logs out of swamps, and was probably quite good at it. However, unfortunately for us, it was too heavy and too powerful to be really good as a mountain climbing snow tractor. It's three man cab was set at the very front of the machine, with the driver seat in the center and a passenger seat on each side. The engine, a big Chrysler V8 industrial engine, was behind the cab, in a box in the middle of a deck, like a small flat bed truck body. On front was a bulldozer blade heavy enough to be better suited to plowing rocks, stumps and dirt, than snow. I understand, although I never saw them, that in the tail end of the machine was over a thousand pounds of lead blocks to balance the excessive weight of the plow blade. With it's full length crawler tracks, it looked almost as rugged as an army battle tank. The Tucker on the other hand looked tall, awkward and fragile with all sorts of mechanical linkage beneath the cab. Looks were deceiving however. It was as sure footed as a mountain goat on deep drifted snow, and had pulling power all out of proportion to its appearance.

The plan was that Phil would plow with the Bombardier, and I would follow and stay in sight with the Tucker. If he got stuck, I could pull him out, and after he finished plowing, It would be a lot easier to climb back up the Mountain in the Bombardier with the Tucker towing it. In deep snow the Bombardier could almost go by itself, but a little strain on a tow chain avoided a lot of wallowing around.

Phil started down the road, plowing small drifts as he went. I learned a lot about Tucker Sno-Cats in a hurry. At first glance, the controls appear similar to a car or a light truck, with a steering wheel, clutch and gas pedals, a floor mounted shift lever and a hand brake, a speedometer and the usual small gauges. Note that I didn't mention a brake pedal, because there isn't one. One was not needed, however, because the hand brake was very effective. People not used to driving a Tucker tend to waste valuable seconds in an emergency pawing around with their foot looking for the non-existent brake pedal. Later, I learned that when Norm drove the Tucker, it was a good idea for me to be in the front seat with him so that when he started looking for the brake pedal, I could pull up on the hand brake. The speedometer is re-marked to indicate that it reads two and a third times actual speed and distance. The big difference is not apparent until you try to make a sharp turn. The front pontoons do not steer individually like the front wheels of a car, but rather the whole axle pivots in the middle. The rear axle also pivots in the middle at the same time in the opposite direction, so it steers very much like a timber skidder, except for another important difference. Unlike a skidder, the power steering is not powerful enough to be moved when the machine is standing still. Also, there is a definite limit, based on hydraulic pump capacity, of how far the steering wheel can be turned with each turn of the engine. Some people say, "You need a ten acre field to turn in." That is not strictly true. The machine can turn in a surprisingly small circle. What is true is that you cannot instantly go from a straight line to a sharp turn, or from a sharp turn to a straight line. You have to plan ahead. I have seen Phil turn the old Tucker around in the width of a two lane road, between a rock wall and a drop off. It did take quite a few reversals to do it, however.

As we descended, Phil made short work of a big drift at six and a half mile, just above the top of the cut off trail. Cragway grade required about an hour of plowing and backing, plowing and backing, getting stuck and having to be pulled out, plowing and backing, plowing and backing. There was no attempt to dig down to bare ground, only to cut a notch in the side slope of snow to provide a level surface to travel on. Most of the afternoon was spent plowing five mile grade, with me watching from a distance, enjoying the scenery, and just generally getting familiar with the road. At one point, the engine stalled and I couldn't start it because the battery was dead. The problem was that the old fashioned vacuum tube two way radio was almost too much for the old fashioned six volt electrical system to keep up with. It was necessary to leave the engine idling at least 1500 rpm to keep from running the battery down. "No problem," said Phil as he got a hand crank out of the tool box and inserted it under the radiator. The well cared for engine sprang to life at the first pull of the crank, and Phil got back to work after reminding me to keep the hand throttle pulled out most of the way.

Late in the afternoon we reached the bottom of the cut off trail. We had accomplished what we had set out to do. We turned the machines around, and hooked a chain from the drawbar of the Tucker to the front of the Bombardier. The trip back up to the summit was uneventful with the late afternoon sun tinting the few high cirrus clouds which were starting to appear. On the summit, we unhooked the chain, Phil parked the Bombardier in the garage in Yankee building, then came into TV for a cup of coffee before heading down for the night. Phil told us that given a reasonably firm surface to work on, the Bombardier is quite a capable machine. Also, with the Bombardier, Parker claims the unofficial Mount Washington snow tractor record of twenty seven minutes base to summit. As the brilliant colors of the sunset shone in the kitchen window, Phil remarked that he would like to get below timberline at half way before dark. He put his coffee cup in the kitchen sink, took a quick look around the engine room to see when the next oil change would be due on one of the main engines, then put his coat on and left. One hour later, just as the sunset colors had faded to blackness, he called on the radio to report, "Safe and sound at the base."

CHRISTMAS ON
MOUNT WASHINGTON

From our kitchen window, through clouds and blowing snow, we can see no further than a tower guy wire about thirty feet away. Anywhere else, it would be considered a raging blizzard, but here the weather is just not that unusual. Light snow has been falling all day and moving around in an eighty five mph wind at twelve degrees below zero. Although some snow drifts from ten to twenty feet deep against the sides of buildings, most of it blows away into the ravines. Inside the WMTW-TV transmitter building, the day is not that much different from any other. We have no difficulty maintaining a comfortable sixty eight degrees in the living quarters. We don't even hear the more than hurricane velocity winds because of the thick walls and the low hum and rumble of the equipment.

On Thanksgiving and Christmas we and our next door neighbor the Mount Washington Observatory crew get together for a turkey dinner with all the fixings. It is our way of compensating for being away from our families on these holidays. Due to the difficulties of transportation, we work a one week on, one week off shift with two of us on at a time. The Observatory, a separate company, also works a similar shift with two or three men on at a time. At Thanksgiving we cooked the turkey and the

Observatory crew did the trimmings, so now at
Christmas the Observatory crew will do the turkey,
stuffing and gravy, and we will do the rest.

Television sign on at 5:15 to 5:30 a.m. went
smoothly, the equipment is all running well, so I have
my breakfast of canned fruit, cereal and coffee. Then
I bake two of our frozen ready to bake pies, one apple
and one blueberry, and get out a package of extra
sharp cheese to thaw. We have several flavors of ice
cream in the freezer. Soon, the pies are cooling on
wire racks in the kitchen counter, and the place begins
to smell a bit like Christmas. Through the morning,
I make the routine checks of the transmitters which
are our reason for being here, and the diesel electric
power plant also in the TV building, which powers
everything on the summit. Some snow is blowing in
through an air vent in the transmitter room and
melting on the floor, so I keep a mop and wringer pail
near the vent and try to keep the puddle confined to
a small area. The engine room is best described as a
winter wonderland, with snow sticking to walls,
ceiling, pipes, wires, in fact everything except the hot
parts of the engine that is running. There isn't much
that can be done about it until the wind changes. I
reflect that if it were a gasoline engine instead of a
diesel, the ignition system would have shorted out
long ago. I peel and cut up a squash to have it ready
for cooking later. Just after 12;00 noon, the night
shift man, Willie Harris, gets up, we wish each other
a Merry Christmas, and he prepares his breakfast of
orange juice, boiled eggs, toast and coffee. Willie,
originally from Philadelphia, Pennsylvania, has
worked on the Mountain for many years, first as a

Stage Driver, then a Weather Observer, before coming to work as a TV engineer. He is an expert skier, and a jazz drummer in addition to holding the highest class of amateur radio operator license. I have a pepper steak sandwich and a cup of coffee for lunch while Willie checks the weather and the status of the equipment. He describes the engine room in ski report terms, "four inches of fresh powder on a two foot concrete base."

We exchange a few comments about probable road conditions in the valley, and how one of the advantages of this job is that we only have to drive to work once every two weeks, which almost makes up for the difficulties of the last eight miles in the company snow tractor.

The 'phone rings, and I answer it. It is Greg Gordon at the Observatory. He tells us that there will be two of them at the big meal. The two friends they were half expecting decided that the weather was too bad to hike up, and a lost hiker has been found safe in the valley. Greg says he will bring the turkey over a few minutes early and John Howe will take care of the 6:00 p.m. observations and the 6:30 radio contacts.

Willie offers to do the dishes if I will do the cooking, so I peel the potatoes and onions. We discuss a green vegetable, and decide to heat up some frozen asparagus. Now everything is ready except for starting each thing cooking at the right time so they will all be ready at about 6:30.

At 6:00 p.m. I find a two foot high snow drift in the entryway which has blown in through the crack around the door. I shovel that out and turn on the yard flood lights. There is no point in shoveling the small drift that is outside the door, as it would drift back in less than half an hour.

Working together, Willie and I set the table and stock it with olives, celery, mixed salted nuts, cranberry sauce, milk, and three kinds of pickles including hot cherry peppers. Greg arrives with the turkey, and we help him find the necessary serving pieces. I mash the potatoes and squash, plug in the coffee pot and set all the vegetables on the table. Soon John Howe arrives, we sit down and Greg prays a short but moving blessing. We all serve ourselves as Greg carves the turkey. We exclaim over how well everything has turned out, as we eat enormous helpings. Soon the main course is history, and we bring out the pies and coffee. Over desert we reminisce over times past and tell stories in which time and fallible human memory has blurred some details and exaggerated others. Many of these stories have been written elsewhere, and some will never be written because they are too embarrassing to the people involved.

Willie tells about skiing down the Auto Road, hitting clear ice, then bare pavement. John Howe recounts a winter when one of the observers, Casey Hodgton of Gorham, left his Volkswagon on the summit too late in the season and had to have it towed over deep drifts by the TV station's Tucker Sno-Cat. My one contribution to all this lore is as follows. Christmas eve, 1968, Mechanical Engineer and snow tractor driver Phil Labbie of Berlin, was taking me down in the new Thiokol Spryte. The wind was sixty to seventy mph at ten to twenty degrees below zero, visibility was fifty feet in clouds and blowing snow.

At six and a half mile, Phil was attempting to plow the drift which normally forms at that point. He got onto the rocks at the edge of the road, and the left track slipped off the front idler wheel. We worked for two hours shoveling and trying to pry the track back on. Finally, we decided it was no use, we would have to walk down. We knew that our radio receiver didn't work, but I hoped that the transmitter might work, so I gave a blind call explaining the situation. Then Phil shut down, locked up, and we headed down the road. At half way, four mile, we saw tracks where our old Tucker Sno-Cat had turned around. We wondered what that was all about, and we kept walking. At one mile we met the Tucker coming up, driven by Phil's son, Larry. Then we got the rest of the story. Willie had herd my blind radio call and called Larry. Larry got the Tucker and started up the road. At half way, he took a good look at the gas gauge, and decided that he had better go back down and gas up, which he did.

Story telling time over, Greg offers to give us some of the left over turkey. We accept a plate of light and dark meat and a small bowl of stuffing which we put in the refrigerator for snacks the next day. After clearing the table, we wish each other Merry Christmas all around, John and Greg leave, and about ten minutes later I turn out the yard flood lights. Willie starts washing the dishes with his handheld two meter radio on the counter beside him monitoring the local repeater. I settle into the big easy chair with my two meter radio beside me in case I hear someone who I want to talk to. The eleven meter sideband radio is on in case my wife calls. She does, and tells me that she and the children are all well. We talk for a while then sign clear, and so ends another Christmas on Mount Washington.

SUNRISE

From time to time the subject comes up in conversation, from what point in the continental United States can the sunrise first be seen. Suggested possibilities are Mount Washington, Mount Katahdin in up state Maine, Cadillac mountain in Acadia park, Quoddy Head, the eastern most point in the continental United States. ' The obvious but not necessarily right answer is Quoddy head. There are three complications to this. First, the time of the sunrise at a mountain west of the eastern most point is actually the time the sun rises over the horizon many miles east of the mountain. The second problem is what high points are in the way of a clear view. The third problem is the sun rises from different directions at different times of the year.

The second and third complications requires careful study of maps. The first complication is mostly a mathematical problem. Knowing the radius of the earth, it is a matter of simple arithmetic to calculate the point at which a line of sight from a know elevation is tangent to the sea level surface over open ocean. Over land, high ground near the calculated point of tangency will move the sunrise point closer to the mountain. Higher ground closer to the calculated point will be the point of the sunrise if it is high enough.

From Mount Washington the calculated distance to sea level tangency is ninety seven miles. A circle drawn at that distance cuts the shore line at Hampton beach 158 degrees from the mountain and in Muscongus bay 108 degrees from the mountain. Open ocean is not actually visible through that whole arc, but the ground that prevents it is not very high. Muscongus bay is about fifty seven miles west of Cadillac mountain. The calculated sight distance from Cadillac mountain is forty eight miles which puts the sunrise 105 miles or 2 degrees 7 minutes of longitude or 8 minutes 26 seconds earlier on Cadillac mountain than on Mount Washington. So we can cross Mount Washington off the list of possibilities for earliest sunrise.

Cadillac Mountain has a clear view of open ocean all the way round to south west from eighty degrees, so an ocean sunrise is visible from there from September fifth through April eighth, but this is not necessarily where the sunrise appears first.

The whole area around Eastport is low ground. The nearest 250 foot contour is twelve miles west of Quoddy Head, so probably the sunrise horizon is about ten to twenty miles from any good viewing point. The big problem is Grand Manan island which is Canadian. Most of Grand Manan is over 250 feet high and therefore blocks the sunrise form Quoddy Head between 98 and 160 degrees or from October eighth to March seventh.

The southern most point of Cutler can see the sunrise past the south end of Grand Manan from October fourteenth to March first. Cutler Point is east of the forty eight mile circle from Cadillac Mountain, but a line drawn south from Cutler Point at a right angle to the direction of the sunrise falls inside the forty eight mile circle by seven miles at least and by eleven miles when the sunrise from Quoddy Head disappears behind Grand Manan. Therefore it would seem safe to state that Cadillac

Mountain has the first sunrise from October eighth to March seventh.

The summer season is a bit more difficult because due to the northern position of the sun it may involve Mt Kathdin. The calculated sea level horizon from Mt Kathdin is eighty nine miles, but at no point is the ocean that close, so all sunrises are seen over land of varying elevations. From due east to about seventy five degrees the circle falls over ground of about five hundred feet elevation which moves the circle in to about eighty five miles. From seventy five degrees to about forty eight degrees the ground level at the approximate distance varies from one thousand to eighteen hundred feet which results in a horizon distance of about seventy two miles

All summer from March seventh through October eighth Quoddy Head has a clear view of sunrise, but somewhere around eighty eight degrees, March twenty seventh to September seventeenth it becomes iffy whether Quoddy Head or Mt Kathdin is first. Between April sixteenth and twenty second and between August twenty second and twenty eighth, due to increasing high ground in that direction from Mt Kathdin, there is some question about which is first. Between April twenty second and August twenty second, there is no question that Mt Kathdin is first.

All of this doesn't consider the effects of atmospheric refraction which will make the sun appear earlier than its calculated time. Atmospheric refraction, the mirage effect varies with temperature and barometric pressure. For celestial navigation there are tables and formulas available to calculate this, but close to the horizon it is difficult to get much accuracy, and downward look angles from the top of a mountain are like, don't even try unless you really have to do it. Anyway, the effect varies all over the place on a short time basis, but at any given hour the distortion is probably about the same from different points within a one hundred mile radius of each other and so will cancel out.

Another variable is that when laying out lines on a map, some things which can make a big difference are only a few feet difference in viewing angle, the exact slope of a hill between contour lines, a few trees on a ridge line, or a small gap between hills that isn't clearly shown on a map. Because the azimuth angle of the sunrise is different for each day of the year, one answer won't do for all year. The only really right answer is to have two or more observers with accurate time pieces stationed at likely points on the day in question. Even this can't be completely right for the reasons stated in the last paragraph, and a cloud in the wrong place at the critical time changes everything. With all of that, the answer obtained by actual observation is valid only for that one day and the other day of the year that the sun has the same azimuth angle.

In conclusion, my best guess is that the first rays of the sunrise arrive at Cadillac Mountain all winter from about October eighth to March seventh and Mt Kathdin is first from April twenty second to August twenty second. Quoddy Head is clearly the first to see the sunrise from March seventh to March twenty seventh and from September seventeenth to October eighth. From March twenty seventh to April twenty second and from August twenty second to September seventeenth the best comment that I can make is that Quoddy Head is a lot easier to get to than Mt Kathdin to see the sunrise. In any event, Mount Washington is way too far west..

RADIO COMMUNICATIONS

Why? Why do we go to all this trouble to operate a TV transmitter on the mountain that is famous for the "world's worst officially recorded weather?" Why put the transmitter in a place which six months of the year can only be reached by snow tractor , and with great difficulty. Of course, the transportation problem is the reason why we have to go to the expense of a full time staff at the transmitter site in an age when almost all other transmitters are unmanned, and run by remote control. The reason is that the radio frequencies that are used for TV broadcasting travel essentially line of sight. They do bend a small amount, but not much. They also reflect, but that usually dose more harm than good. Therefore, the higher the transmitting antenna is placed, the more homes will be able to receive it's signal. This is why many TV stations have towers fifteen hundred to two thousand feet high. These are not cheap to build either. The WMTW-TV 8 antenna is seventy feet high on a fifty foot tower on a 6254 foot high base. Its a couple of hundred feet from the 6288 foot high summit. This puts out the signal one hundred miles or more in most directions, but still if you live in a deep valley behind a hill, you are out of luck.

Here is some background information. The AM radio broadcast band is .5 to 1.5 megacycles, now called megahertz, abbreviated MHz. These radio waves tend to follow the surface of the earth, and so the system works best if the transmitting antenna has a really good electrical ground. Low swampy ground is good, a salt marsh is even better. At night the signals bounce off the ionosphere, a layer in the upper atmosphere at the edge of space, and can be received thousands of miles away. This is called skip. Citizens Band (CB) is about 27 MHz and works about the same way except that its longest skips from the ionosphere happen in the middle of the day. Amateur radio operators have studied this from the very beginning of the radio age, and by choice of time of day, and frequency between two and thirty MHz, and considering other factors such as sunspot activity, are able to communicate around the world with very little transmitter power. Until the invention of satellite communications, all long range commercial communications was handled by commercial radio operators using the same principles that amateurs use. The TV broadcast band starts out with channel two at 54 to 60 MHz where skip doesn't happen often enough to be useful except as a novelty. Channel eight is 180 to 186 MHz.

In the 1930s when the Mount Washington Weather Observatory was first established, at about that time   Edwin Armstrong was in the process of inventing frequency modulation (FM) One of the purposes of the observatory was to research 50 MHz radio propagation In those days 50 MHz and above was unexplored territory. Partly as a result of these tests, Armstrong built the Yankee Radio Network which pioneered FM radio broadcasting. On the summit in 1938, he built Yankee Building and the old Yankee Power House to house one of his stations.

The so called Alford tower, which for many years supported the standby TV antenna which was made by Alford company, was originally the FM radio station antenna tower. Old pictures of the summit show the 50 MHz antenna which used truck spring leaves for radiating elements. When FM broadcasting began to be a success, General Sarnoff of RCA, in order to run Armstrong out of business, was able to get the FCC to change the frequencies assigned to FM broadcasting to the present band of 88 to 108 MHz. But that's a whole other story in itself. When Mount Washington TV Channel 8 was formed , they bought the Yankee Radio Networks interests on the summit in order to have a place to build the TV station.

Because of the line of sight nature of the higher radio frequencies Mount Washington has always been a desirable location for radio and microwave repeaters. Channel 8 leased space in it's buildings to just about every service both private and government that you can think of to name off. Surprisingly, the one service that most people would think of first is the Telephone Company. They do not relay from the summit to anywhere else. Their microwave system from Littleton to the summit is just to service the telephones on the summit.

On the roof of Yankee building is a forest of two-way radio antennas, and numerous microwave dish antennas are mounted on the walls facing outward from the summit. There are more dishes on the south end of the TV building, and still more on a mounting frame outside the old Yankee Power House. There are even a few side mounted on some of the towers. The Auto Road Company in the Stage Office and the Observatory in the State Park building also have more radios and repeaters. A long time ago I gave up trying to count how many transmitters and radio frequencies are in use on the summit.

The down side of all this is a thing called intermod which is short for intermodulation. When things go wrong, two radio frequencies can mix and produce two other frequencies, the sum and difference of the original ones. These intermod products can mix with others and with other frequencies, and .... Well, anyway the possibilities stagger the imagination. In a place where we have as many frequencies in use as we do on the summit, a computer program will print out an unbelievably long list of things that theoretically could happen. The one thing we have going for us is that most of them won't happen, or at least not until it will cause the most consternation. Intermod products can happen any time that pieces of different kinds of metal are in loose contact in a strong RF (radio frequency) field. Piles of junk, loose tower hardware, abandoned wires, cables, and feed lines are prime examples of this. All of which is a great incentive to keep transmitter sites neat and well maintained. Here is an example of what can happen. One morning I got a 'phone call from one of our radio customers, Stewart Shaw of Berlin NH. He said, "I've got a wicked intermod problem on one of my repeaters, it started about eleven last night. Did anything change up there at about that time?" I told him, "I don't know of anything except that there is a big piece of construction machinery parked outside that wasn't there when I went to bed last night at nine last night. Maybe you've got a signal reflecting off the side of it, or maybe its got a radio in it that is stuck in the transmit mode." Stewert came up to deal with the problem. He noted that the big machine was an excavator which belonged to Dan Taillon, one of his radio customers. It did have an antenna on it but no radio. Apparently Dan has antennas and mounting frames on all his machines, but only a few radios, so he can quickly put a radio in any machine he is using if he needs it. Stewart tried everything he could think of with no help. In desperation, grasping at straws, he removed the antenna from the excavator and the problem disappeared. He put it back and the problem was back. He removed it again and called Dan Taillon to tell him to leave it off until he got that machine off the Mountain. Now how could an antenna with no radio on it cause all that trouble? My guess is that the feed line with nothing hooked to it, we call that unterminated, was exactly the right length to resonate at what ever frequency would do the most harm. But that's just a guess. With intermod problems, if it is not a real problem in a radio, you move a piece of junk or tighten a loose bolt and the problem goes away, it usually doesn't pay to spend a lot of time trying to figure out exactly why.

Another problem is strong local signals getting into and overloading sensitive equipment. One classic example of this is a tourist in the parking lot picking up an FM radio station on his hearing aid. In the early days of portable TV cameras and home TV cameras the video tape recorder was a separate unit carried as a back pack or a tote bag. The five feet or so of connecting cable picked up everything it shouldn't have, and it was extremely difficult to use one on the summit without having Channel 8 programming mixed with whatever one was trying to record. The modern camcorders which have the video tape recorder in the same small unit as the camera, and no dangling cables almost never have this problem. Over the years I have solved many problems of this kind by simply hunting up all the screws that hold a case together and being sure that all the panels are closed and connections tight. Another standard cure all is to wrap things with kitchen aluminum foil. This does work but it requires frequent adjustment and retuning.

In modern times all communications to and form the Mountain is by radio or by microwave, there are no wire lines to the summit. When I first came to the Mountain in 1964, the Observatory maintained a series of survival shelters along the road at half mile intervals above timberline. These had old fashioned crank telephones in them and the Observatory crew worked very hard to maintain a line connecting them to the Observatory. Every thunderstorm that happened, and we have a lot of them, the lightning would take out sections of the line. This system, and the shacks are now gone, partly due to the difficulty maintaining them, but mostly because people now days do not appreciate survival shelters in the wilderness, and the vandalism problem was getting out of hand. In the 1870s the Army Signal Corps had a telegraph line to the base. Some of the old steel core wire can still be found among the rocks. I have no idea how much trouble they may have had maintaining that system when it was in use.

Until sometime in the 1970s there were not dial telephones on the Summit. There was in the cellar of the old Observatory a 'phone company microwave system to Littleton NH. The equipment was made by a company that went out of business a long time ago. It Provided four channels for four old fashioned crank telephones. These are called ring down circuits. The Observatory had a 'phone and a Civil Defense hot line. The Hotel, which was not yet the State Park, had a 'phone and a pay 'phone. That was it. TV did not have a 'phone except our own system to the studio which worked on a subcarrier of one of our microwave systems. This system was in use long after almost everyone else in the country had dial tone, and fewer and fewer telephone operators knew how to deal with it. Someone in New York or further away would dial "Operator" and say, " I want Gorham NH. zero one." The operator would say something like, " That isn't a real 'phone number and if you had the right number you should be able to dial it direct." After quite a bit of discussion involving the supervisor and the supervisors supervisor, finally someone would call the Gorham operator who would say, "sure I'll put it through."

Even though it went by microwave, the TV 'phone system worked just like any other crank 'phone system. One ring for the transmitter, two rings for the studio and three rings for the Chief Engineers office. To call outside, we would ring the studio, have them dial the number, then throw a switch to connect the two systems. For incoming calls the studio would ring the Mountain and throw the switch. Either way when we were done with the call we would have to call on a two-way radio link, "KCD539 this is KCD540 clear the 'phone please." Then Master control at the studio would open the switch and ring a short ring to let us know that it was done.

KCD540 was on a commercial frequency in the broadcast auxiliary service, 26.13 MHz, just below the CB frequencies. It never worked as well as it should have, and we tried a variety of things for antennas. The best working one was when one of our radio customers abandoned a piece of high quality coax line which ran to an antenna shack one hundred feet from the TV building. I rigged up an antenna in the cellar of the shack with a nine foot length of number fourteen electrical wire from the center conductor to a nail in a beam and two more lengths connected to the braid and laid into the rocks. When the telephone company Updated their equipment and we were able to have our own line with dial tone, the 26.13 MHz system was abandoned. I took over the antenna for CB use with a bit of retuning. On and around the Mountain there has always been quite a bit of activity in amateur radio and its "black sheep" cousin citizen band or CB as it is commonly called. At risk of having fellow amateur and commercial radio operators throw rocks at me, I say that CB does have it's place in the communications world, and I have been involved in it from the very beginning in the early 1960s. I had a CB sideband radio on the Mountain, and another one at home, so that my wife and I could call each other in the evening without running up a big 'phone bill. After I talked to my wife I would answer calls from anyone else in the North Country who wanted to talk to me. I was amazed to find that even though the antenna was down in the rocks on one side of the Mountain, it seemed to receive and transmit signals equally well in all directions. There is some principle of radio propagation there that I never was able to figure out. My wife never was comfortable with the system because too many people knew when I wasn't home, so we had to be careful what we said. We eventually abandoned the system for that reason.

One summer our vacation relief man was John Wilcox, NS1Z, a very active ham radio operator. He talked me into and helped me modify the shack antenna into a ten and twenty meter dipole for use on the amateur bands. I have an Atlas 210X radio which is a neat little rig. Five band, two hundred watts PEP sideband power. It was one of the first all solid state radios that was any good. With this I was able to talk all over the eastern half of the United States, and hear people as far away as the West coast, South America, and Europe. I am not very aggressive at calling people so I never completed calls more than a couple of thousand miles.

For many years, my shift partner was Willie Harris, AG1Z, of Jackson NH. originally of Philadelphia. He and I were quite active on the two meter band. On the summit, two meters has a couple of drawbacks. One is that on many channels it is possible to key up two or more repeaters at the same time. This can get confusing to say the least. The other is that many radios do not have the selectivity and filtering that they should have, so with all the commercial frequencies in use they go into receiver desensitization. From time to time various people have installed two meter amateur repeaters at the Observatory, Due to intermod and other forms of interference it is usually necessary to use tone squelch. The upside is that on a high point like Mount Washington, if everything is just right, some things can work remarkably well. We found that with Willie's Yaesu handheld at the kitchen window with a rubber duckey antenna and low power, one tenth of a watt, he could solidly work the Mount Greylock repeater in Western Massachusetts, 141 miles away.

In 1979, Chuck Martin, WA1KPS, owner of Tufts Radio Supply in Boston loaned us a ten GHz radio. He and Wayne Green, W2NSD/1, publisher of 73 Amateur Radio Magazine were involved in pioneering this band for amateur radio. This was a whole different experience in radio communications. The radio itself was an aluminum box about eight inches square and about four inches high with a feed horn antenna on one side. The feed horn resembled a square funnel about five inches long and about four inches square. There was just two controls, an on/off/audio gain and a frequency adjustment. A headset with a boom microphone plugged in, and that was the whole thing. I don't remember what it used for a battery, but it wasn't much. It only made about fifteen milliwatts of power, that's fifteen thousands of a watt. That was power enough that we were able to communicate over a one hundred mile distance with dead full quieting, meaning no hiss or noise in the audio and full duplex. That means just like a telephone, no switching between receive and transmit. I marked lines on a piece of shirt cardboard based on map data that when it was placed on the kitchen windowsill they pointed out the mountains where we expected that Wayne and/or Chuck would go to try to call us. We found that if the edge of the box was lined up with the appropriate line it got us the best signal every time.

Amateur radio operators are identified by call signs issued by the Federal Communications Commission, and when meeting each other in person they usually introduce themselves by first name and call sign, as,

" I am Martin, N1ARY." We also like to make up phonetics for the call sign which may be different from the ones in the official phonetic alphabet. The reason for the made up phonetics is that they stick in peoples minds better than the real ones. A few examples, AG1Z " Always Grabbing One Zipper" K1OIQ " Keeping One Observer In Quarantine" KS1S " Keep Singing One Song." The correct phonetics for me would be "November One Alpha Romeo Yankee" but I use "Number One Amateur Radio Yankee." There is a story to how my phonetics were suggested. Shortly after I had upgraded and got my new call sign, and before I had thought about it, two long time friends of the Mountain visited. They were Ken Thompson, K4RO, "Radio operator" and Eunice Thompson W1MPP, "Madam Pickle Puss." They were two old time Western Union telegraph operators and it is my understanding that they were at one time the oldest amateur radio couple in the world. It is also my understanding that Eunice was the first woman amateur back in the days that women were discriminated against in the amateur world. But when she called in Morse code how could anyone tell? It was Eunice who said, "Well obviously AR is Amateur Radio." So that is how I got my phonetics and my tie to history. Ken and Eunice are both dead now, or as we say, they are Silent Keys. The last time I saw them she stood as straight and strong as a telegraph pole and he just sat in a chair and looked sick, but he out lived her.

Once upon a time there were about six people sitting at the table in the TV building. Danny Johnson from the State Park was the only non amateur in the group. Someone walked in and introduced himself by name and call sign. We all introduced ourselves the same way. Danny looked puzzled, he didn't have a clue what was going on. After everyone else had spoken he said, "And I am Danny Johnson from the State park, I don't have any letters or numbers or anything."

A BEAUTIFUL DAY,
A BEAUTIFUL TRIP

For thirty eight years, my life has been divided into two parts. For eight days I am on the Mountain tending the big transmitters, and for six days I am a country boy, a home owner and a family man. Here is one of the more memorable adventures of my other life.

One day my wife suggested "Why don't we sometime visit a friend of ours in Lexington Massachusetts?" The friend was John Perjemski, a photographer who had hiked the Mountain a lot in winter and also had visited us at home. She noticed that the map showed an airport close to his home, so she said, "why don't we fly there." I said, "Why not." Then I got to looking the situation over. The airport was Hanscom Field a big airport with a control tower located near Boston, and in under the edge of the Boston TCA (Terminal Control Area.) All my flying had been done in the North Country where most of the airports don't have control towers, and the few that do are staffed by down home type of people who have the time and patience to deal with light, slow moving aircraft. The rule was that you had to have a transponder to enter a TCA, and most light aircraft didn't have them. The TCA has been described as like an upside down wedding cake, a series of concentric circles, the smallest one extending from the ground up, and the larger ones starting at some altitude and extending upwards. I went out to Fryeburg Airport and spoke to Jim Beyers, the flight instructor. I showed him the map and asked, "Do I understand correctly that I can get into Hanscom Field by staying below this altitude past this point?" He said, "Sure that's just how it works, no Problem." The next day was forecast to be clear and beautiful, so I asked him to reserve N78179 for me all day tomorrow. Then I went home and called John Perjemski to ask if he would be home. He would be and he agreed to meet us at Hanscom Field at a certain time.

The next day dawned clear and beautiful as forecast. The plan was that our four year old son would stay with my mother that day, and we would take our three year old daughter, Anita, with us. We went out to the airport and I proceeded to untie the tiedown ropes on the aircraft and check all the things that need to be checked before flight. N78179 is a 1969 Cessna 172 Skyhawk, dark blue and white paint job, high wing, four seats, 150 hp, cruising speed 110 mph. It would cruise at 120 mph if the wheel fairings were installed, but us country boys don't like wheel fairings, they make it difficult to inspect the tires and brakes, and they can collect mud and snow which can freeze the wheels. Landing on bare pavement with wheels that you didn't know were frozen is the sort of thing that can really grab your attention. With just the three of us and no luggage we were way below allowable gross weight, so we hand pushed the aircraft over to the gas pumps and filled the tanks. This was before child's car seats were as highly developed as they are now. We had a home made booster seat which we used in the car. We set that in the back seat, set Anita in it and fastened the seat belt. She could see out the window, and was in the same seat that she always rode in. I filed a flight plan by telephone, and soon we were on the way. The flight plan is not required, its only purpose is if someone later reports you missing, Search and Rescue has some idea where to look and what they are looking for.

As we climbed to altitude we found that the weather really was as beautiful as it had been forecast. In those days the primary radio navigation system for light aircraft was the VOR system. My plan was to fly inbound to the Manchester VOR then outbound on the Manchester 185 radial to Hanscom Field. Because it was a short trip with plenty of gasoline, clear daytime weather, over mostly populated areas, it was not necessary to do a lot of complicated arithmetic. We just spotted landmarks on the ground and checked them off on the map as we passed them. Over the hills of Wolfeboro we hit a few bumps in the air, nothing serious, it just kicked the tail around a bit. I looked back to see how Anita was handling it, and she was just looking out the window just as unconcerned as could be.

When we got to Massachusetts we found that on the ground as far as the eye could see was divided highways with cloverleaf intersections, and housing developments jammed in between. Neither the Aero chart or a road map gave any hint of what a bowl of spaghetti the freeways are in that area. It was hopeless to try to match up anything on the ground with what the map showed. But no matter. The radio navigation had done it's stuff and Hanscom Field was visible straight ahead. I had to use five different radio frequencies in short order. (1) Manchester VOR (2) Automatic Terminal information Service, which gives a recorded message of wind, temperature, altimeter setting, and all the routine stuff that the controllers don't want to have to repeat to everyone (3) approach control (4) control tower, and (5) ground control. After we landed and taxied clear of the runway, a yellow truck with a big lighted "follow me" sign led us to a parking spot. After we shut down and climbed out. I locked the doors and took the key with me which seemed like the thing to do in a big city parking lot. The "follow me" truck took us to the terminal building where John met us. He took us to his home where we had a really nice visit. He is a professional photographer. Every place in his home that there was a place to hang a picture he had a very large color picture he had made from pictures he had taken. His father, who owns an upholstery business, had found that when old roads were being rebuilt, he could have all the old cobblestones that he could truck away. Thinking that they may be worth something someday, he had most of his house lot covered with big, neatly stacked piles of cobblestones. I made the remark "In an artillery attack, this would be the place to be, behind all these piles of rocks." We reminisced about old times on the Mountain for a while, then John took us back to the airport. The "follow me" truck took us out to the aircraft and the driver told us, "When you are ready to taxi, call ground control and I will lead you out to the runway. When I leave you, switch to the tower frequency." We did that. I noticed that the place was a lot more crowded than it was when we landed earlier. There were airplanes all around us, mostly heavy piston twins and bigger. We got in line, did what we were told, and after a while we were airborne. Shortly after takeoff, the controller called, "Cessna 179 turn right NOW!" Controllers don't usually show much emotion in their voice, so I caught the tone of urgency. Instantly I rolled that old Skyhawk into the tightest turn that I dared to with the airspeed and altitude that I had to work with. Then I answered the radio call and he told me to switch to departure control. After we turned about ninety degrees, I rolled out of the turn, continued to climb, and switched to departure control frequency. Departure control was so busy that I couldn't get a word in edgeways. I never did see what almost ran over us, I had too many other things to pay attention to. Obviously the controller misjudged how slowly a light piston single would depart (Airspeed for best rate of climb 85 mph) and so he cleared for takeoff something a whole lot faster too close behind us. When we got to 1000 feet altitude, I sat there, microphone in hand waiting for a chance to check in with departure control. I wondered, "What do we do now. Oh well, at least we seem to be headed out of this mess." When I was sure that we were out from under the Boston TCA, I trimmed for climb and turned to fly inbound to the Manchester VOR. As we gained altitude we spotted Mount Washington on the far horizon 120 miles away. Now we can see where we need to go, we don't need the radio navigation or anything else. I stopped tracking the VOR and headed for home. After we crossed the state line into New Hampshire the congestion on the ground thinned out somewhat and we were able to spot things on the ground that we could check off on the map as we passed them.

Then we had another idea. I am not sure who thought of it first, but we said, " before we go home lets take a ride up around the Mountain." I thought, " Why not, it's a beautiful day, a good running airplane, plenty of gas, and we are in no hurry anyway. Also we have the airplane all day so we have to pay for three hours engine time whether we use it or not." We climbed to 7500 feet and circled the summit, being careful to approach it first with the wind behind us, and staying further away than a lot of people do. Now I do a bit of mental arithmetic to figure out how many feet per minute rate of descent will get us from 7500 feet down to 1500 feet in only 24 miles. I work it out and reflect that that is the only mathematics that I have had to do all day. There is a small clearing in the woods, possibly a swampy area, which is about two miles west of Fryeburg airport, and just the right place to start an approach into the pattern. It is a lot nicer navigational check point than some unidentifiable highway intersection. I got down to 1500 feet within a quarter mile of the clearing, close enough. I call on the radio, " Fryeburg Unicomm, Cessna November 78179 two miles west landing at Fryeburg, over." No answer. That's not unusual at small airports. As I turn into the downwind leg of the pattern I check the windsock to be sure that I am doing the right thing. On base leg, after checking carefully to be sure that no one is coming in on a long final, I call, "Fryeburg traffic, Cessna November 78179 is entering a short final for 32 at Fryeburg, Over." No answer, I didn't expect one, but if there had been anyone else around, they would know where I am and what I am doing. They could either stay out of my way or ask me to stay out of their way. That's the way it's done at small airports. It sure is good to be home and out of the crowds and confusion of the big cities. We land, taxi to a parking spot, shut down, and fasten the tie down ropes. Then I read the engine hour meter to figure how much the rental fee is. We go into the administration building, and Jim Beyers is there. We pay for the flight time and tell him about our trip. We then get into our car and head for home, the finish of a beautiful day and a beautiful trip.

WIND CHILL AND OTHER WEATHER IDIOSYNCRASIES

"I am not now and never have been intentionally in the weather business." That is what I have said many times when I have been accused of being a meteorologist. People I meet in public places recognize me from that brief weather report which I have given for many years on Channel 8, and so they think of me as a "Weather Man." They also think that I work for the Mount Washington Observatory, which of course I don't. One person challenged me with, "Just how much formal training do you have in weather?" I told her, "Not one bit." "Hmph." she said as she stomped off in disgust, her suspicions confirmed.

However, over the years I have learned a few things about weather. As a Maine backwoodsman, I have always had to keep an eye on the sky and try to guess what is going to happen next and what I am going to have to do about it. As a licensed airplane pilot it is necessary to know a little bit about the environment in which airplanes operate. Working on Mount Washington, we are exposed to some highly concentrated forms of weather. Everything we plan on doing is prefaced with the remark, "Weather permitting" and most of the time it doesn't permit.

WIND CHILL

On Mount Washington the temperature is usually low and the wind is usually high, frequently high enough to be downright dangerous, so the concept of wind chill catches the popular fancy. The way it has been explained to me, the wind chill chart was developed by Doctor Paul Siple in Antarctica in1945. The maximum wind that he had to work with was only thirty five mph. The published charts only go to fifty mph. The range from thirty five to fifty mph being an extrapolation of his data. It was his contention that the curve flattened out at high wind speeds, and so above fifty mph it doesn't matter how much higher the wind is. Those of us who commonly experience one hundred Plus mph winds disagree. As I see it, it is a matter of heat transfer. You are trying to maintain body temperature with cold air taking heat away. Anyone who knows anything about heating, ventilation and air conditioning knows that heat transfer is directly proportional to air flow. The textbooks don't say anything about heat transfer tapering off at high speeds. Anyway, when someone asks me a question like, "What is the wind chill at one hundred fifty mph and twenty below zero," all I can say is that it is nine inches beyond the edge of a six inch wide chart, somewhere beyond ninety below. The point is that at high wind speeds, wind chill factor is at best a guess. It's best use is to show the need to be careful. Another use is to explain to people in the valley why the work they want done outside is going so slowly. Obviously thick dry warm clothing properly worn is the most important protective factor. There is an old Scandinavian saying, "There is no such thing as bad weather, just inadequate clothing." There is a lot of truth to that although the Mountain does push it a bit. Another consideration is that it is the wind that reaches you that matters, not the wind that is measured at the top of the observatory instrument tower, unless of course you are up there.

On the ground, in the shelter of rocks, buildings, snowdrifts and such, which is where you will be if you have any sense and can do it, There will be a lot less wind than the officially reported figures. Wet clothes are a disaster, and so far as I am concerned wind, cold and blowing snow is a lot harder to deal with than wind, cold and dry air.

Another question which is sometimes asked is "Does the wind chill apply to motor vehicles?" The standard answer is, "No." However that is not completely right. If a vehicle has been parked outside all night, twelve hours or so, it will have cooled off to whatever the temperature is, and it doesn't matter whether or not the wind is blowing. What is a consideration is that when a warm vehicle is shut off it will reach the outside air temperature sooner in a wind than it will in calm air. The wind chill chart is not intended to be used to figure this, so you are on your own to guess how fast a vehicle will cool off. The only other light that I can shed on this is that when I was in the U.S. Air Force in the early sixties, and of course on an air force base the wind is always blowing, The rule was that in the winter vehicles that are needed should be started and idled for fifteen minutes every four hours. When I started working on the Mountain, if it was necessary for the old Tucker Sno-Cat to stay overnight on the summit, it would be left idling all night. The new tractors all have electric heaters that can be plugged in. That is of course the best answer to the problem both on the Mountain and anywhere in the North Country.

WIND

The thing that Mount Washington is most noted for is wind , and lots of it. The highest wind ever officially recorded at a surface recording station (watch out for those qualifying statements) was recorded on Mount Washington in 1934, 231 mph, but that was a one time event. The highest wind that I have ever seen is 175 mph. I have gone between buildings in a 124 mph wind, at forty six below zero and I can tell you that wasn't easy. Anything over 100 mph is difficult and dangerous. The year round average wind is thirty five mph, so it doesn't take checking weather records to guess that the wind is up around seventy mph as often as it is nearly calm. Everything on the summit has to be engineered for wind loads that are normally unheard of except by aircraft designers. When I walk around outside, I use an ice chisel for a walking stick. This is a tool with two inch chisel blade on about four feet of three quarter inch pipe. It weighs about five pounds. When I drive that into the ice, it goes where I want it to and stays there. Winter hikers use an ice axe or ski poles for the same purpose, but an ice axe is too short to be an effective walking stick, and ski poles blow around in the wind too much. We have a couple of cheap motorcycle helmets on a shelf in the TV living quarters. People ask about them, and my comment is, "A common industrial hard hat Doesn't stay on your head very well in a one hundred mph wind." We use these when we have to de ice microwave antennas in bad weather.

Although the TV building is very strongly built with thick walls, and there is a constant dull roar from the diesel generators in one end and from the transmitter cooling blowers in the other end, we are aware of high winds outside. When the wind is near one hundred or higher, we can feel a shudder in the building and hear bits of ice ranging from small pieces to multihundred pound chunks hitting the outside walls and roof. In gusty winds the pressure changes can cause an uncomfortable pounding in our ears. One night as I lay in bed trying to sleep, I heard a loud clanging and banging outside. I knew what it was, there was a stack of empty fifty five gallon drums just outside my window, and they were blowing away. The noise continued for a long time, as I wondered how long it would take for them all to depart the area. The next morning, one of the observers told me that one of the drums had got caught in a whirlpool of wind between the TV building, the Old Observatory, and the Old Yankee Powerhouse. It had spun around for about an hour before it left. When things blow away on the summit they usually don't go very far. Those oil drums all ended up in the rocks within one hundred yards of where they started from. One of the weather observers lost his hat, a knitted watch cap, from the top of the instrument tower in a 120 mph wind. I found it a couple of days later 150 feet away.

During the construction of the new summit house, a hurricane struck. I am not sure what winds were recorded, probably over 150 mph. At one point the bands broke on a load of three quarter inch plywood. Someone who saw it said that it reminded him of a giant dealing a deck of cards. A full size aluminum trailer truck box trailer was blown over on its side, and later the same day the wind changed direction as winds do when a hurricane passes, and the trailer was blown back onto its wheels. Except for damage to the side of it and things inside, it looked like nothing had happened.

People ask if we use ropes to get between buildings, the answer is, no, they would ice up too much.

ICING

Four facts: (1) Five days out of seven year round

average the summit is in clouds. (2) The average temperature is twenty nine degrees. (3) The average wind is thirty five mph. (4) The bad side of the above, these averages tend to happen together.

When moisture laden air is blown against solid objects in below freezing conditions, the moisture freezes on contact, forming rime ice, also called impact ice or frost feathers. The way it works is that the air being lighter turns and goes around the object, but the moisture droplets being heavier go in a straight line until they hit the object, where they freeze in place. Rime ice builds up first and fastest on small objects and sharp edges. So when we go into clouds, we see the icing first on guy wires, then on building corners, then on the edge of every shingle. It is important to understand that rime ice builds up on the windward side of things, unlike drifting snow which collects on the downwind side. This is why it forms sharp points and fine detail, sometimes resembling the feathers of a birds wing. This material is pure white in color, and about the composition of hard packed snow. It has been known to form as fast as six inches per hour and extend as much as twenty feet from structures. Rime ice doesn't form very much when it is snowing or blowing snow because moisture which has already frozen into snow flakes doesn't stick as much.

The other type of icing we encounter is called blue ice or clear ice. This is solid chunks of water much like the ice cubes in your refrigerator. This happens when the summit is below freezing but there is rain coming from a layer of warm air above. Blue ice does not form on sharp points and small objets as much as rime ice does. Unless the wind is very high it tends to do a more even coating of things. Combinations of blue and rime ice can do several different things, mostly bad. Rime which forms over blue ice can be stuck on pretty hard and be real difficult to get rid of. Blue ice which forms over rime is unstable and can break off in hard multihundred pound chunks which can do a lot of damage if they hit something. A mixture of blue and rime ice can be very thick and lumpy, again very dangerous to get hit with.

For us, an interesting characteristic of ice is that radio frequency energy passes through ice like it wasn't even there, but liquid water blocks the energy. All of the various types of antennas on the summit are inside radomes of some sort so the ice doesn't form directly on the radiating elements. We can have thousands of pounds extending ten feet or more from a radome with minimum effect. Sometimes very lumpy blue ice will reduce signal levels somewhat, but I think that is a focusing effect something like the lumpy glass that is sometimes used for bathroom windows. If we have a buildup of rime ice and it starts to rain, the rime will soak up water like a sponge, and we will see a sharp rise in reflected power. The reflected power will be worst just before the ice drops off. A radome with no ice but wet with rain may show more reflected power than when it is covered with many feet of rime ice. This can lead to another problem. A microwave system which several days in a row, usually in the spring time, quits working in mid afternoon and comes back by itself in the evening. In a microwave system the radio frequency energy goes between the equipment and the dish antenna through a waveguide which is a precision made hollow pipe. If it gets water in the waveguide through a leak, the signal is cut off. When the water freezes the signal goes through as though nothing was wrong.

What can happen is that through the winter moisture gets in and freezes, and we don't know anything about it. In warm weather in the spring, when the sun hits the waveguide, it thaws the ice and cuts off the signal. When the sun goes down the water freezes again, allowing the signal to pass. When we figure out what is happening, we have to take the system apart and dry it out by pulling rags through the waveguide with a stiff wire, and blowing warm air through it with a hair drier. Of course the whole problem could be avoided by pressurizing the line with dry air or nitrogen, but that would require fixing the leaks, which is where the moisture gets in in the first place.

One last thought on icing. The words light, moderate, and heavy do not lend themselves to exact meanings, and what the observatory calls light would be called heavy on an aircraft. The observatory's moderate is beyond an aircraft's range of stay out of there.

Snow

Mount Washington does get a lot of snow, and most of it is moving horizontally so fast that it is difficult to tell whether it is new snow falling, or at least trying to fall, or snow that fell yesterday coming back after a wind shift. With the winds we commonly experience on the Mountain, snow doesn't generally stay in one place very long. It doesn't stay on high spots but it fills in low spots and accumulates on the downwind side of everything. It will also find it's way in through the smallest opening in buildings, vehicles and clothing. It doesn't seem to me that it matters on the summit whether we get a little bit of snow or a lot in any given year. The snow fills in and drifts up in all the standard places, then it doesn't much matter how much more we get, it all goes elsewhere. It does matter down on the road however. Snow shoes are seldom necessary for a few hundred yards around the summit because the snow is usually wind packed so hard that it is necessary to step hard on your heels to get a grip. One thing people have trouble understanding is that it is a lot easier to deal with a one hundred mph wind if the wind was one hundred fifty last night than it is to deal with a fifty mph wind if the wind was thirty last night. The reason is that in an increasing wind, loose snow is picked up and blows around cutting visibility, filling in tracks and just generally making things miserable. In a decreasing wind all the loose snow has found a home and will stay there, at least until the wind shifts. No matter how bad conditions are due to blowing snow and fog we can usually find our way around the summit without too much difficulty. On the shift change trip, once in a while we have turn around and go back down. Sometimes we will sit in one spot for several minutes trying to catch a glimpse of any rock or post or anything that will give us a clue to move a few more feet. This is not always due to just snow. It can be a combination of snow and fog and lack of contrast in a condition known as white out. Sometimes this necessitates having someone get out and walk in front of the tractor to find the road. And some people think I am kidding when I speak of visibility limited to the back side of our own plow blade.

CLOUDS AND FOG

Five days out of seven the summit is in clouds. Technically that isn't right. Officially the definition is that where a cloud touches the ground, it is fog. It seems to me that with clouds whipping by at high speed, and visibility rapidly changing back and forth between fifty feet and fifty miles the distinction gets a bit fuzzy. Many years ago, I brought my parents up the Mountain for a visit. My mother remarked that standing in the wet clouds or fog reminded her of being hit with wet bed sheets hanging on a cloths line. That's about all that can be said for being socked in. On the two days out of seven when we are not in the fog, we get some very unusual views of clouds in action. Everyone understands an overcast, but we get some rather close up views of the bottom of a cloud layer. The thing we have that is specific to mountain tops (and airplanes) is an undercast. We may have clear sky above, or we may have all sorts of clouds around and above us, but an undercast is a layer of clouds below us which we are looking at the top of. Sometimes it will be a broken undercast, with areas where we can see valleys below. Sometimes just the peaks of the high mountains show through, but the most spectacular ones are the ones where the cloud layer is complete for 360 degrees around us, and it is just below the summit, so we are standing on the only solid ground that can be seen for a hundred miles in any direction. If there is very much wind, the top of the undercast may not be level but will show contours roughly following the contours of the ranges below. One scene that is interesting to watch from our kitchen window is an undercast forming on one side of the southern peaks, but not on the other side, then the clouds flow over the peaks like water flowing over a dam. Watching this process from above has given me an insight into a remark made by one of the old Aircraft Mechanics at the airport. Referring to flying VFR (Visual Flight Rules) he said, "Don't ever try to sneak up through one of the notches underneath an overcast. You may find yourself boxed in with no place to go." From the things that I have seen here, I can also agree with another of the old Mechanics remarks "The weather is usually different on the other side of the mountains."

In order to understand some of the things that we see from the summit, it is necessary to know what clouds are and why they are. Air contains water vapor which is invisible unless there is more water than the air can hold in which case some of the water forms droplets which can be seen, and that is what cloud or fog is. The colder it is, the less water the air can hold as water vapor. There are two ways to measure this. Relative humidity is the percentage of water that is in the air of what it could hold at the present temperature. As the temperature goes down and the amount of water remains the same, the relative humidity goes up. Dew point is the temperature at which relative humidity reaches one hundred percent and clouds form. When air rises, the atmospheric pressure decreases. The air thins out, a given amount of air takes up a larger space. The amount of heat in the air remains the same, but because it is spread out more, the temperature goes down. This is why in the summer time it is common to see rising columns of air form puffy white clouds with the bases all at about the same height. The cloud bases are at the altitude where the temperature has dropped to the dew point. The same thing happens when the wind blows over mountains. The air rises to pass over the mountain, it reaches a certain height where it's temperature reaches the dew point, and a cloud forms. As the air goes down the other side of the mountain, as it reaches lower altitude, the temperature increases, and the cloud droplets disappear into water vapor. This is what lenticular clouds are all about.

From a distance you may think it strange that with a high wind blowing, that one cloud stays in that same spot all day. From close up, you can see the cloud form on one side, and disappear on the other side. This is the reason that many times the summit of Mount Washington will be in clouds when there is not another cloud anywhere in the North Country. When flying VFR I like to know what the dew point is. Then with ground temperature and a simple calculation, I know at what level clouds may form. Alternatively, by checking the outside air temperature gauge (thermometer) I can tell where I am in relation to the cloud forming altitude. If there is dust particles in the air, water droplets can collect on them and form rain drops or snow flakes, but that is a whole other story.

Sometimes drifting snow can be seen extending in a plume from the top of the Mountain, this should not be confused with clouds.

*Mount Washington as seen from the scenic turnoff
in North Conway*

*The Thiohol Spryte working 25 to 30 feet above the road
surface just above half way.*

The Tucker Sno-cat

The Bombardier Muskeg Tractor

Fourteen feet of rime ice on TV antennas

Rime ice on two-way radio antennas on Yankee Bulding

The TT-10/25 1954 TV Transmitter

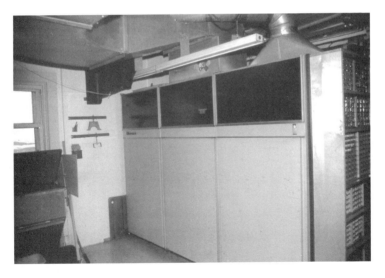

The TTG-17H 1981 TV Transmitter

The HT-20 HS 1997 Harris TV Transmitter

The Weather Set

The Old Switchgear

The New Switchgear

The Old Engines

The New Engines

The summit from the air

Left: Donald Gauthier
Right: Martin Engstrom

A BAD TIME FOR SHIFT CHANGE

Tuesday morning in February, 7:23 AM, the bedside 'phone rings. I wasn't planing to get up until eight or nine AM. I groggily answer the 'phone on the first ring and Dick Cushman, my boss, says, "Oh, did I wake You?" I answer, "Yeah," and he says, "Well I guess that makes up for the times you've done it to me." He is joking of course, we are all professionals who don't mind being woke up when there is a problem, in fact we are more upset if we are not awakened at the first sign of trouble. He explains that Don Gauthier had a relative die and he would really like to get off the Mountain early, and could I come to work a day early? I think fast. Of course I really don't want to come to work a day early, but Don filled in for me recently, and I know that he will be chain smoking and pacing the floor, and his wife at home is probably doing the same. I say, "Well, I can't make it to the base by nine AM, maybe ten or eleven." Dick says, "Ok , make it eleven AM." My wife, Rosalie says in a panic, "there is a storm coming!" I reassure her that we will not take any unnecessary chances, and anyway the storm shouldn't be that much of a problem today. After hanging up the 'phone I reluctantly get up and get dressed for the Mountain. After breakfast it does take a while to wrap up the affairs of the week and get ready to go to work, but I am able to leave the house shortly after ten AM. Paul Clark meets me at the base with the snow tractor. The trip up is uneventful in nice weather. Clouds close in and light snow is just starting as we arrive on the summit. Don tells us that it was not his uncle who he expects to die at any moment, it was his wife's brother, forty two years old, who just keeled over unexpectedly. Paul and Don head down, and Bill Ingals and I settle in to tending to routine business, and waiting for the shift change Wednesday morning. We telephone Paul the weekly grocery order which I would normally pick up. The snow gets more intense and we settle into one of the major storms of the winter.

The next morning, Wednesday, our regular shift change day, as I am tending the routine morning chores, Russ Heald, who is coming up to replace Bill calls. He says that he had a car accident in Standish Maine on the way to work, and that he, "probably won't make it to work today." It seems that someone plowing a driveway cut across the road in front of him unexpectedly and Russ hit the snowplow truck broadside. Russ says that he will have to make arrangement to have his car towed. I ask him if he is hurt and he says that he is not except that his chest hurts, probably from the seat belt/shoulder harness. I ask him if he is going to a doctor or an emergency room, and he says that he isn't sure. He is obviously too shook up to know just what he is going to do next, so all I can do is hang up, and notify Dick Cushman.

On the Mountain, conditions are not all that great for a shift change. At eight AM the Observatory reports that we have ten inches of new cold, dry snow that blows around like feathers. Twelve hours ago the wind was from the south east, but now it is from the south west at fifty gusting to sixty five mph. This means that the snow landed in one direction and is now being picked up and blown in a different direction. Shortly after the eight AM radio contact, Ken Rancourt from the Observatory starts down with the Observatory tractor to do the shift change. About eight thirty Ken calls to report that he doesn't know where he is. He thinks that he is in the vicinity of the tank farm about four hundred yards from the summit. Most of the time visibility is so bad that he can't even see the back side of his own plow blade. He will try to turn around and find his way back to the summit. Half an hour later he does make it back to the Observatory. Ken calls us to tell us that he will wait until about noon to make a final go/no go decision. There is some discussion over telephone and radio as to whether or not Paul should work awhile plowing the lower half of the road. It is decided that it would be a whole lot smarter to just wait awhile and see what happens. About ten a.m. Ken decides that if the wind and blowing snow do calm down enough to make the shift change possible, it will be too late in the day to be fooling around trying to do it. Therefore it would be best to cancel it now so that everyone involved can get on with the work of the day.

Now the next question is what are we going to do for the rest of the day? When a shift change fails, morale hits a low understandably. Everyone has completed the work that they had planned for the week, and no one feels like starting on something new only to have to leave it for a week. So nothing except routine operating work is going to get done anyway. Ken suggests, "Why don't we get together for supper tonight?" He says that he will do a beef roast and vegetables, we can do the dessert and coffee. When we do a meal together we always do it at TV because we always have to have one man in the building at all times, but at the Observatory, after their six p.m. observation and radio calls they don't have to have anyone around until the nine p.m. observation. It is moderately tricky to carry a hot roast beef and freshly cooked vegetables one hundred yards through blowing snow in a seventy four knot (eighty five mph) wind, but it is nothing that hasn't been done lots of times before. We have quite a bit of cake left over, so Bill bakes a batch of cookies. During the six PM news we prepare a batch of coffee, set the table, and turn on the yard flood lights. The guys from the Observatory come over and a good time is had by all, except for a couple of low points. They tell us that Mike, who was supposed to come up today, also had a car accident with a snow plow on the way to work. Bill informs everyone that Don Gauthier called to tell us that the uncle he had been expecting to die did die Tuesday night.

Thursday morning I tend to the routine morning duties, Ken starts down and Paul starts up with Russ and Dick Cushman. I wake up Bill to get ready to go home. This whole morning feels weird. I keep thinking of things like, "I haven't done my laundry and made my bed yet. No, wait a minute, I don't have to, that chore is a week away." We hear various radio conversations between Ken and Paul. Apparently they are having a very difficult time plowing huge drifts in five mile grade. The trip up which would normally take one and a quarter hour, takes three hours. When they arrive, Russ fills us in on the details of his accident. His car was heavily damaged but he is all right except for a badly bruised chest from the seat belt/shoulder harness and lots of other minor aches and pains. The police did call a rescue unit to take him to a hospital, so he did get checked thoroughly.

Dick wants to do some work on the summit, and Paul wants to do some more plowing, so Paul takes Bill down, and comes back to get Dick. They head down and a couple of hours later Paul calls to report "Safe at the base." Then Russ and I settle into the routines of the week.

BROKEN GUY WIRE!

Nine a.m. Thursday morning December seventh. From the east window of the transmitter room, I could see that we were in the clear with blue sky above. At eight a.m. the Observatory had reported that we were still in the clouds with one hundred feet visibility, as we had been continuously since arriving on the summit yesterday morning on our shift change. The whole west side of the building including our kitchen window, from which we enjoy one hundred thirty mile views on clear days, was solidly iced up. There is not much point to deicing the window until the clouds clear, the icing stops, and there is something to see. Now it would be worth doing. I open the inner window and the inner storm window which gives me access to the outer storm window which is quarter inch thick Lexan, the same stuff that airplane and racing car windshields are made from, the only thing we have found that is tough enough to withstand the windblown chunks of ice which are common here on the summit. I pound forcefully on the inside of the outer storm window with my clenched fist, and success! The ice dropped of to reveal blue sky and sunlight, and,? What's this? On the ground beneath the window were coils of heavy steel cable. About twenty feet from the building and just to the left of the window is a massive block of concrete which is an anchor for two of the guy wires for the main TV antenna. Most of the time, the only thing which can be seen from this window through the fog is the guy wires disappearing up to the right. Now the top one is missing. I can see that it is still attached to the anchor. When I put my cheek to the window and look up to the right, I can see the end fitting still attached to the antenna, and that is all, the wire has broken at the very top. As soon as I collect my thoughts, I call my boss, Dick Cushman, and he begins to make plans.

The main TV antenna structure consists of a fifty foot high tower on a heavy concrete base, with a sixty five foot high antenna mounted on top of the tower. The structure is designed to be self supporting and would not need guy wires in the valley where very high winds are not expected. Here on the summit that is not good enough, so to provide extra strength to withstand the kind of winds we experience about one hundred days each year, there are three pairs of guy wires spaced one hundred twenty degrees apart. The lower wires going to the top of the tower are one and three eighth inch diameter steel cable, and the upper ones going to the top of the antenna one hundred fifteen feet above the ground are seven eighth inch diameter steel cable. It is one of these upper ones that has broken. When the wind blows it tightens the wires on the windward side and slightly loosens the ones on the lee side. The looser wires tend to flex more in gusty winds and therefore are likely to break sooner. Most of the high winds we get are from between west and north, and the wires by the window are south east. Now that one has broken, it could indicate that the others are reaching the end of their useful life.

Dick orders new guy wires, but it will take a couple of weeks to get them, and we don't dare to wait that long. We will have to do something temporary. There is no way to get to the top of the antenna, so we will have to get a crane or a helicopter. A helicopter powerful enough to lift two men in a work cage and the end of a guy wire at this altitude is expensive to rent, and if the weather will not allow the work to be done, we would still have to pay a lot for the chopper and crew to come and stand by

The next day, Dick and Paul Clark, our driver/ mechanic, bring up Dan Taillon, owner of a local crane company, in our brand new Piston Bully snow tractor. Plans are made and they go back down, plowing snow out of the road as they go. Dan has one of his men buy tire chains for all wheels of one of his truck mounted cranes, and meet us at the base. They tow the crane up behind the Piston Bully and by shortly after dark the crane is safely parked on the summit.

Saturday December ninth, two days after the broken guy wire was discovered, Dick, Paul, Dan, and his son, and two men from Savino Tower Company in Connecticut come up with the material for a temporary guy wire. At eight a.m. the temperature is seven degrees, the wind is from the west at sixty to seventy five mph and visibility is one hundred feet in clouds and blowing snow. No good for what we have to do. Luckily, by the time the crew is ready to work, we are in the clear and the wind is down to ten mph. The crane will barely reach a foot or two above the top of the antenna, and it is some kind of a trick to lift two men and the end of the temporary cable on a single crane line, but that is how they do it, and in a few minutes the cable is hooked on and the men are safely back on the ground. It is then no big deal to fasten the temporary cable to the anchor and pull it as tight as practical. Everything is done by two thirty p.m. I cook up a big kettle of beef noodle Hamburger

Helper, and the crew has a quick lunch before heading down the Mountain. The immediate emergency is over and the crane is left on the summit to put up the new guy wires when they arrive.

Sidelight: after the crew leaves Don Gauthier, my shift partner, discovers that the main fuel shut off valve for the diesel electric generating plant, a lever operated valve, is half closed. He opens it and we wonder what that was all about. We speculate that when Paul ran an air hose out to the guy anchor to operate an air wrench he must have hit it. That could have been quite a problem, to lose all electrical power due to fuel starvation, then try to figure out what the problem is. We notify Dick and Paul, and tie the valve open to avoid this problem in the future.

SEQUEL #1

December thirty first, the new guy wires are delivered to the Glen House and we haul them up to the summit in the Piston Bully.

SEQUEL #2

January eleventh, it was decided that we would wait until spring to install the new guy wires. Meanwhile, we did not want to Pay rent on the crane all winter. By now there was enough snow in the road that we had given up on wheeled vehicles for the rest of the winter. Dick, Paul, and Dan Taillon thought that with the Piston Bully towing the crane and the Thiokol pushing we could get the crane through the drifts all right, so we tried it. Just above seven mile, at the top of Cow Pasture we found that it just wasn't going to work out, so the rest of the way we plowed with Paul driving the Piston Bully and Dick driving the Thiokol. It was necessary to take the snow right down to solid ice for the crane to have solid footing to roll on. We didn't get off the Mountain until after dark that day.

Sequel #3

June thirteenth, things are just so much easier to do in the summer when wheeled vehicles can travel the road. It is still some kind of a trick to pick a day when the tower crew and the crane and it's crew are available and get them on the way and have the weather on Mount Washington be suitable for the work to be done. Another problem we have to work around is that large trucks can travel the Auto Road only when it is closed to the public. That means the crane has to start up the road before seven a.m. and will not be able to go down until after the night patrol clears the road, about seven' p.m. Dan Taillon has done many jobs on the Mountain, and so he knows all the rules, so this is very little problem. Of course, cars and small four wheel drive trucks such as we use for crew transport can come up or down any time.

Dan and his son bring up a crane which they bought new only a couple of months earlier. It is mounted on a Ford nine thousand series long wheel base truck with a Caterpillar 3406 diesel engine just like our generators. It weighs twenty four tons and the boom can telescope out to one hundred forty feet. Shortly afterward Dick and Paul arrive with three men from Savino Tower Company. The new crane can easily position a work cage with two men in it just where it is needed at the top of the antenna. Again, luck is with us. The wind is calm, which is very rare, the temperature is thirty eight degrees, and it is clear to ninety miles visibility. It doesn't take very long to drop the tops of the old guy wires, and hoist up and connect the new ones. There is quite a bit of work on the ground, disconnecting the old and connecting the new at the anchor points. Then the new wires have to be tightened to twelve thousand pounds tension, and a transit is used to be sure that the antenna is perfectly vertical. While the tower crew is doing this, Dick and Paul have Dan hoist them up in the work cage to remove various pieces of electrical conduit and other no longer needed junk from the TV standby antenna. After lunch, Dan repositions the crane for the tower crew to install a new radome on the WZPK-FM STL (Studio to Transmitter Link) microwave dish. Sometime during the winter, ice had destroyed the radome. Fortunately, it did not damage the dish or the feed horn, so service was not interrupted. All in all we had a very successful day. The only sour note was that someone had bought a bowl of chili at the State Park cafeteria and had thrown the whole mess, plastic bowl, spoon and chili right in the middle of the windshield of Dan's new crane. Paul had to get the soap sprayer to clean it off. We speculate that it was some hiker who didn't like to have to walk an extra couple of hundred feet because we were blocking part of the hiking trail. Anyway, the work was all done and Dan was ready to take the crane down as soon as the night patrol cleared the road.

THE SLIDE SHOW

A few months after I started working on the Mountain, George Holden, of Holden Brothers Chevrolet, asked me if I would do a talk for his Lions Club meeting. I told him, "I really don't know much about doing that sort of thing." He said, "Oh, don't worry about it, you'll be among friends." So I said, "Well, ok." I spent the next two weeks wondering about it. "How am I going to do this, what am I going to say?" I had taken quite a few slide pictures on and around the Mountain, so I picked out some and arranged them in a slide tray for my projector. A slide presentation can get quite dull when the slides are in random order, so I tried to follow a logical order, at the Base, up the road in winter, inside the buildings, around the summit and back down the road. I figured that I could talk for a while, and when I ran out of things to say, I would show the slides. Mr. Holden invited my father to come with me. Came the big night, I put on my best suit and off we went. Everyone treated us very well, we had a good meal, then I talked for about half an hour and showed the slides. It all worked well and was well received.

Later, someone who had been at the Lions Club meeting asked me to do a show at another organization, then another, and another, and another. I found that I was more comfortable to go directly into the slide show with very little introductory talk, then have a question and answer period after. I would end by saying, "And that concludes my show, if anybody has any questions I will try to answer them." Each time I did the show I would think of improvements that could be made, so I would take more pictures and add the ones that seemed best. I always kept the same format of a trip up and down in winter. Someone once asked me if the show had a title, so I said, "A Winter Trip on Mount Washington," so that has been the title ever since. I learned just how to word certain remarks to get the best laugh.

As the years went by the slide show was my ticket to many interesting adventures, and sometimes I was able to take one or more of my family members with me. We got to meet many interesting people and see lots of historic buildings and towns, and sit in on business meetings of all sorts of organizations. When I was dating my wife to be, I took her to one of my slide shows, trying to impress her. It turned out to be a class reunion for a school that had gone out of business fifty years earlier. There was no one there less than about seventy years old, and some may have been ninety to one hundred. Any entertainer will tell you that these old timers do enjoy the show, but you can't get an audible laugh or any reaction out of them. Its the hardest work there is for an entertainer. My wife to be was impressed anyway. After the first few I started charging, and gradually increased the price to keep the quantity of requests down to what I could comfortably handle.

Wylie Apt Jr., "Bunkie," of North Conway asked me to do a show for his aviation club meeting at Hanscom Field in Massachusetts. I told him, "I have to go to work Wednesday morning, I can't drive home from Massachusetts that late at night on a Tuesday night." He called back later and said, "We've got a deal for you, we'll send a limousine to take you there and bring you back, and we'll pay you twice your usual fee." I agreed and that was the way we did it. It was a big deal for me, but in all fairness it wasn't that big a deal for the club because Tom Harris of Harris Taxi Company in North Conway was a member and was going anyway. He simply drove his limousine instead of what ever car he would have taken. One highlight of the evening was that as I was approaching the door of the building with my hands full of slide show, an Air Force Captain in full class A uniform held the door open for me. Quite a thrill for a former Air Force enlisted man.

For many years I used an old Sawyers 500 projector which I bought when I was in the Air Force. It was a good machine in it's day, but that was forty years ago. One of the replacement bulbs that I got for it had a slightly different part number, but was supposed to be interchangeable. It had a little reflector inside the glass envelope behind the filament which the others didn't have. After I did a show with this new bulb, when I shut the machine off, I noticed an orange glow coming out of the ventilation slots. I looked closer and saw that it was the condenser, the big plus lens between the bulb and the slide, was glowing red. I thought, "I never happened to notice that before, oh well, I guess its all right." The next show was at the Falmouth Fire Department. When I set up and tried to focus, the picture appeared broken into blocks. I shut down, pulled the cover off the light box and looked inside. The condenser was broken into twenty or thirty pieces but still holding together and in place. I had to borrow a projector to do the show. I was unable to get a replacement condenser, so I bought a Kodak Carousel with auto focus, remote control and a zoom lens, and several trays. The new machine intimidated me because it had so many mechanical complications that looked like they could break down in ways that could be difficult to fix. When I bought it, of course I bought a couple of spare bulbs for it, and I asked the clerk if I needed to have a spare drive belt on hand. He told me, "No, that's not a thing that you could change while an audience is waiting for the show." That didn't help my confidence in the new machine.

About the second or third time that I used the new projector was at a restaurant at the north end of Franconia Notch. When I tried to set up, the motor wouldn't run. I stuck the blade of my jack knife into the cooling slots and found that the fan did have torque on it but not enough to run. My worst fears confirmed, too complicated a machine to be dependable, Someone who lived close by had a simple projector, and someone who lived further away had a carousel. They both headed out. When the simple machine arrived, I started hand feeding slides. The colors didn't look good, but I thought, "Its a low powered bulb, that's all." About a third of the way into the show the Carousel arrived and we set it up. It didn't work just the way mine didn't. Then someone in the kitchen called out, "By the way, that outlet is on a dimmer." They brought the voltage up and the projector worked fine. Afterward I thought about keeping a voltmeter in my kit, but I decided against it. Now that I know what can happen, I won't be fooled that way again.

I did a daytime slide show at the Western Electric factory in Andover, Massachusetts. The person who contacted me had an office which was a cubicle among hundreds of others, just like the Dilbert comic strip. Deep within the factory they had an auditorium which was a full size movie theater. They asked me if I would like to use their projector. I said, "My slides are in Kodak Carousel trays." They said, "We can handle that." They took the trays up to the projection booth and gave me a clicker to change slides with. I don't know how it worked, I didn't have to point it in any particular direction, it just worked. What was even more amazing, there wasn't a microphone or a speaker to be seen anywhere, but everything I said was amplified for the audience, and if anyone in the audience asked a question, it was also amplified. The system was absolutely perfect with no distortion or feedback. I thought, "Leave it to the 'phone company to know how to handle audio." I don't know what kind of a projector they had or what it's light source was, but my slides never looked better or brighter, and they were shown filling a full size movie screen. After the show, after most people had left, a few gathered around to ask a few more questions. There was a young lady who seemed to be waiting for something, but didn't have a question. It turned out that she was to give me a guided tour of part of the factory. But she wasn't just a tour guide, she was an Engineer who had set up a production line to automatically assemble and test printed circuit boards. It was interesting to see the automatic machinery that placed parts on the boards. I had never before seen a wave soldering machine in operation. After they paid me for the slide show and gave me a good lunch in the cafeteria, as I headed for home, as I crossed the state line into New Hampshire, I reflected that it was all very interesting, but it was good to be out of the land where they drive with more enthusiasm than finesse.

The Maine Snowmobile Association wanted me to do a show in Bangor. I told them that I couldn't drive that far and back in one day, and it would cost them a lot for mileage. They said, "No problem on the cost, and we will pay for you and your wife to stay in the hotel that night." We had a fine trip up and back, and the show was well received. U.S. Congressman Jim Longly was there, and we had a long talk, not about politics. He had been a Communications Officer in the Marine Corps, so we had mutual understanding and interests as we were both former military electronics troops. He told me about his cell phone. He said, "See this antenna? Its a fake, the real antenna is a piece of wire molded into the case, and this flip out thing to talk into? Its fake too. The real microphone is this little hole in the main case." Apparently he had taken it apart to find out how it worked. I thought, "It is rare to find a big timer like this who knows anything about the high tech gadgets that he uses."

The engine temperature light came on as I was almost at the top of the Kancamagus Highway. I had a slide show at a women's club meeting over in Vermont. I had allowed plenty of time to travel, I wasn't too concerned about it. I figured that the engine had simply overheated in the climb, and would cool off soon enough as I was gearing down the other side. So I continued the last hundred yards over the top, shifted into low gear and closed the throttle for the long descent into Lincoln. After quite a few miles the light was still on, and I was getting close to the point where I would have to step on the throttle to maintain speed. I pulled into a rest area, opened the hood and let it cool a bit before opening the radiator cap. Now I had a problem, I had nothing to carry water with. I looked in a trash container, and there right on top was an empty one gallon spring water jug, just like a plastic milk jug. I said a brief prayer of thanks to the lord for providing for my needs. It may seem like a small thing, but that empty plastic jug was the one and only thing which I desperately needed at that point. It was spring and all the roadside brooks and ditches had plenty of water in them. I filled the radiator and it leaked like a sieve. "Oh oh, now I really am in trouble." I thought "Well all I can do is go as far as I can go and fill it again." So that is the way I proceeded. I found that I could go about five or six miles between fill ups. All the while torn between two thoughts. One, to get to the slide show and two, I am liable to ruin this engine by running it red hot and filling it with ice water. At one point I saw very fresh moose tracks where I obtained water. I made it to my destination in plenty of time. As I sat at the head table, I felt something on my neck. I caught it, it was a wood tick. It must have gotten on me at one of my water stops. So I sat there with a tick in my hand. As it nibbled at my finger tips I wondered how to get rid of it. The floor was carpeted so I couldn't just step on it. Finally I crushed it between two keys. The banquet was good and the slide show was well received. They had offered to put me up in the hotel over night, so I took them up on that offer, then I called home to alert my wife that I would be limping home the next day.

After breakfast, I checked the oil. There was no water in the crankcase so apparently I didn't crack the block with all that ice water. So why didn't I go to a garage and have them install a new radiator? Because I knew that I had at least one used one at home that would fit. I considered having my wife and/or my son bring me a radiator and some tools, but every mile I could make toward home was two miles round trip that they wouldn't have to make. At a gas station I bought two cans of stop leak which did exactly no good. No way was I going to try to make it back over the Kancamagus so I took the southern route. In Ashland, as I was getting water, a young man whose name I didn't get asked if I needed help. I told him my problems and he said that he thought he knew a place where I could get a used radiator cheap. At that point I was getting tired of the whole thing, so I said, "If we can get a radiator, if you would help me change it, I will pay you." He took me to a junk yard, and sure enough, we got a good one cheap. There on the roadside, with just the tools that I had in the car, we changed it. I broke one of the automatic transmission oil cooler lines but this was not as much of a problem as it might have been because I knew something which saved me that day and I pass it along in case it may get someone else out of a mess some day. Those lines are low pressure and it is all right to patch them with a piece of rubber gasoline tubing and a couple of hose clamps. My new friend took me to an auto parts store where I got the tubing, a couple of clamps and a fitting to go into the radiator. Soon I was on the way home with the warning light staying off for mile after mile. That old Chevrolet Impala was as tough as a steam locomotive. This happened when it had about 140,000 miles on it, and when it had 180,000 miles on it and the body had too much rust to patch to get another inspection sticker, The engine still used less than a quart of oil in a thousand miles. It would usually start before it turned over one full turn, and if not handled carefully, it could still lay long smoking streaks of rubber. We sold it to someone who needed the engine for something else.

If it were not for that slide show, I and my family probably never would have gotten to see the inside of some of the big old resort hotels in the area. An Auctioneers convention at Loon Mountain, at the other end of the Kancamagus, had my wife and I stay at the hotel over night. We got to sit in on some of their meetings, which was quite an experience. Washington New Hampshire is a small and very old town on high ground near the Vermont line. There are three big, old wooden buildings side by side on Main Street. They are the town hall, the school, and the church. As I get the story, the three have interchanged the three uses several times in the past two hundred years. Another interesting place where I have done a couple of shows is Weeks State Park off route U.S. 3 just south of Lancaster. This is up on a mountain top. It was the summer home of Senator Weeks. He was the Senator who sponsored the legislation for President Teddy Roosevelt to set up the National Forest. (Just a personal gripe, don't ever confuse a National Forest with a national or a state park, they are completely different.) The last time that I was there, I was introduced to Senator Weeks grand daughter, who is now an old lady.

At the Red Jacket Inn in North Conway, I mentioned that over mountains in high winds aircraft altimeters read incorrectly high. After the show a man confronted me. He flew Orion patrol bombers at Brunswick Naval Air Station. Although he didn't say so in so many words, it was obvious that he felt that a civilian pilot couldn't possibly know anything about flying that he, a professional Naval Aviator didn't already know. I mentioned Bernoulli effect. His expression changed and the color drained out of has face as he suddenly realized the meaning and application of something he had only half heard in school. I can picture him thinking, "So that's why the Mountain looked so close when the altimeter said that I had plenty of clearance." There is another problem which I mention here to anyone who flies in winter. Play with your E6B computer or equivalent and see the effect of low temperature on altitude readings. In normal flying this is ignored because everyone is subject to the same error, so it doesn't matter. But consider this 7000 feet (that's what the instrument says) ten below zero fahrenheit , that's 6300 feet actual altitude. That's below the tops of a couple of towers on Mount Washington. That's not even considering the wind effect that I mentioned earlier. Just one more tip, if you want a close look at the top of any mountain, in addition to not trusting your altimeter, make your first pass with the wind behind you so that if you have misjudged anything, the wind will carry you over the summit instead of pushing you down into it. Also remember that the regulations do say to stay at least five hundred feet away from buildings and people, one thousand feet away from groups of buildings and outdoor assemblies of people. I may not know much about flying, but I do know a few things about mountain flying.

At the Ramada Inn in Lewiston I did a show for a lions club meeting. It was a regional meeting, and the region as I understood it was all of New England, New York State, Quebec, and the Maritime Provinces. The show was early afternoon, so on the way home I decided to stop at Howel's Gun Shop in Gray to buy some ammunition. I seldom go there, so the clerk didn't recognize me. Now you have to get the picture. I was in my best dark suit with white shirt and tie, short military style haircut and spit shined black shoes. I was on an emotional high from being the guest speaker at such a big deal meeting. It was just starting to rain a few drops, so I didn't take a great while walking from the car to the shop door. When the clerk saw me, he must have thought that I was a government agent there to give him a hard time about something. If he were a private in the army and a general walked in, he couldn't have snapped to alert any sharper. I have never anywhere been waited on any quicker or more efficiently than I was that day.

Yes, that slide show has taken me to many interesting places, Introduced me to many interesting and influential people, and led to many adventures.

LOST IN A BLIZZARD
OR PHIL'S MISADVENTURE

Wednesday December 16, 1981, shift change day. The weather was not too bad early in the morning, but we knew that a storm was moving in and would hit about ten a.m. Normally the plan is to leave the base at nine a.m., but this morning all interested parties have been notified to be at the base by eight a.m. The idea is that if the crew can make it to the top, do a quick turn around, and get started down as quickly as possible, it should be possible to get back down below timberline before the storm gets too bad. Phil Labbie of Berlin is the driver. Phil is our company mechanical engineer, handy man, welder and diesel mechanic in addition to being our snow tractor driver and mechanic. He has thirty two years experience on Mount Washington, having worked for the U.S. Air Force jet engine testing laboratory for four years before channel eight started and hired him. Phil's sixty fifth birthday and probable retirement date is only about two weeks away. Art Dunlap and Don Gauthier are coming up for their regular work shift. Dan Theiboult from Berlin, originally hired as summer help, has been hired to replace Phil. He is twenty three years old, a strong, eager and willing worker, but Phil has not done very much to train him as a snow tractor driver. In fact, Dan has only driven the machine around in the flat field at the Glen House. He has not driven it on the Mountain at all. Also along is Dave Schurman, a radio man from Conway. Apparently his plan is to stay overnight to work on

111

equipment on the summit and go down on a trip later in the week. The carefully worked out plans start to fall apart when Phil accidentally locks his keys inside his truck. That problem solved, the trip gets underway forty five minutes later than planned. In retrospect, without that delay the rest of the story would probably have happened about the same way except that they would have made it to the summit and started down with Willie Harris and me instead of Art and Don. We do have radio communications of sorts. We have new U.H.F. handi talkies, one in the tractor and one in the TV station which work through a repeater next door in the Weather Observatory. Also, Dave has a handi talki on a different frequency on which he can talk to his wife in Conway. The trip proceeds normally for about an hour, then Phil calls from Cow Pasture, Seven Mile, to report that he is stopped in very limited visibility, and is trying to see enough to proceed. Shortly afterward he calls to tell us that he is canceling the trip and turning around to go back down. The Observatory next door reports that the temperature is twenty degrees, but the wind is gusting to one hundred forty mph with heavy snow and blowing snow, reducing visibility to the point where the men in the tractor probably can't even see the back side of their own plow blade most of the time. Then Art calls to tell us that Phil, unsure of where he was driving, had stopped and got out to try to find the edge of the road. That was half an hour ago and he hasn't been seen since. That radio call makes everybody really wake up and pay attention because we are all very much aware that with the weather as bad as it is, survival time outside of a heated cab could be very short.

On the summit, about all that we can do is handle communications, but it turns out that in itself is a big job. We notify Chief Engineer Parker Vincent who immediately heads for the base of the Mountain. Don's wife Arline calls, she had been listening on a scanner receiver and heard the whole thing. She understands, but was concerned that everyone in the North Country who has a scanner would know that something was happening, and all sorts of incorrect rumors would soon be circulating. She volunteered to notify Phil's wife, and suggested that I should notify Dan's father. After thinking that over a bit, I called Mr. Theiboult at work and chose my words carefully. I told him, "Your son isn't in any real danger, but you may start to hear all sorts of rumors, so I want to give you the straight word first." Then I described the problem to him in detail. He thanked me, and we hung up. Greg Gorden at the Observatory called his home church to activate their prayer network. George Soblaris, State Police radio man, called to ask what was happening. His first instinctive reaction was to grab his cold weather gear and head for the base, but his second thought was to stay where he was and make 'phone calls to notify persons who could help. This was probably the best thing for him to do. In about an hour there was six snow tractors and about thirty well equipped and experienced men gathering at the Glen House. Motorola Radio Company offered to send a radio direction finder and crew, but this wouldn't have helped any because Phil didn't have a radio with him, and we already knew where our machine was within a couple of hundred feet. It was a foregone conclusion right from the beginning that due to the extreme limited visibility there was no hope of finding Phil. His only hope was that he could find one of the rescue crews.

Meanwhile in the TV snow tractor, Don, Art, Dan and Dave were having troubles of their own. One problem in this sort of operation is when you are able to move the machine, how soon do you dare to? Remember that the lost man may find his way back to where he left the machine, so you must not leave the area too soon. This means staying put for several hours, or until the lost man has been found. A cold, difficult wait. The engine, idling and not pulling a load was not making very much heat. The cab although reasonably tight, could not keep all the cold and blowing snow out in the one hundred forty mph wind. Dave Schurman was not dressed as heavily as he should have been, and was beginning to feel cold. Fortunately, we were getting low on paper towels on the Mountain, and so there was a whole case of them in the cargo. Dave stuffed crumpled up paper towels inside his clothes until he had enough insulation to feel comfortable. Another problem soon appeared, carburetor icing and the air strainer plugging with drifting snow. This was not quite as bad as it might have been however, because on the Thiokol Spryte snow tractor the engine cowling opens up inside the cab, and most engine work is done from the front seats. Driver in training, Dan, had to clear ice and snow out of the carburetor several times in the next few hours. Fuel was not a problem because the machine is equipped with an extra large gasoline tank which is always full when we leave the base.

In the mean time, rescue crews had placed themselves at various places along the road above timberline and below where visibility was just impossible. All they could do then was wait and hope. When it was almost dark, we all feared that we had seen the last of Phil alive. Then came the long awaited radio call from one of the machines in the rescue effort "We have Phil with us." Phil had appeared at one of the tractors at the foot of Cragway grade. He was quickly helped into another tractor one hundred feet away where a medical doctor was waiting for him. The doctor checked him over and gave him some warm sugar water to drink.

The wind had died down slightly, and visibility had improved enough that our crew knew where they were, and where the road was, so they started down with Dan at the controls. Ken Rancourt with the

Observatory tractor was the next one down, so he stayed put until he had our machine in sight, then he started down. At five thirty p.m. everyone was at the base safe and sound. Phil was rushed to Berlin Hospital where he was treated for exposure and exhaustion, and kept for a couple of days. The only injury he got was a little minor frostbite around one wrist, apparently from his watch band. Chief Engineer Parker Vincent treated the rescuers to supper at the Town and Country Motor Inn in Gorham. Among those who helped us with people and equipment were the Appalachian Mountain Club, Wildcat Ski Area, the U.S. Forest Service, N.H. Fish and Game, and others. Currier Trucking used their flatbed trailer to transport snow tractors

AFTERMATH

In the next few days, as stories were heard and compared, the rest of the picture emerged. The road across Cow Pasture just below Seven Mile heads north east for about eight hundred feet across a flat windswept plateau with few distinctive landmarks. Then it makes a curve to the left and heads north west about six hundred feet to Hairpin Turn where it turns easterly. The area north and west of the curve is a gradual slope where, depending on snow conditions and visibility, we have taken short cuts with the snow tractors. Apparently, Phil made the turn to the left about one hundred feet too soon, and traveled two or three hundred feet parallel to the road before he realized that he probably wasn't still on the road. When he got out to try to find some landmarks, he followed the plow blade across the front of the machine, then took three steps diagonally out from the right front corner where a gust of wind knocked him flat. When he got up, he got turned around and never found the machine again. When he realized that he wasn't going to find the machine again, he started diagonally down hill, being careful not to head down too steeply least he end up in the Great Gulf to the north. Somehow he crossed the road between the curve and Hairpin Turn without realizing it, and stayed to the south, up the hill from the road. Several times he laid down to rest, almost gave up, and had to force himself to continue. It was only about a mile from where he was lost to where he was found, but it took him five hours to travel that distance. He found one of the culvert marker poles on Cragway Grade. These are maple poles about twenty feet long, long enough to not be completely buried by the deepest drifts. Then he knew that he had some hope. He followed the poles down to the tractor and rescue crew which reported him found.

Two weeks later, although it was past his retirement date, stubbornness set in, and he came back to drive for us for the rest of the winter. Later, Paul Clark of Gorham, who had ten years experience at Wildcat Ski Area as a driver and mechanic was hired, and Dan Theiboult was promoted to Transmitter Engineer to replace Willy Harris when he retired. Our best snow tractor has a properly mounted radio in addition to the drivers handi talki. Both tractors have one hundred yards of nylon line on a reel mounted in the cab so when anyone gets out to look for the road he can tie on and be able to find his way back to the machine. On exposed stretches of the road we set trail marker posts about fifty feet apart on only one side of the road to eliminate uncertainty about which side of the posts to travel on, and a distinctive double post at the turn where the trouble started. We are a lot quicker to call the trip off if the weather is bad, and most of us make it a point to have a radio in our pocket when we are traveling on the Mountain.

About a month later on January 25, 1982 a member of a search and rescue crew was killed looking for two winter hikers who had done all the standard stupid mistakes, but that's another story.

PANIC IN THE ENGINE ROOM

Shift change day, Wednesday, January 25, 1984, 7:35 a.m. Suddenly the lights started to go out. At a Diesel powered site such as Mount Washington, when an engine shuts down, the lights do not go out instantly. The engine takes a few seconds to coast to a stop, As the lights dim, all the sounds in the building also taper off and are soon replaced by the steady ringing of alarm bells, and the dim glow of emergency lights. At the first sign of trouble, I head for the engine room as I had so many times before that fall and winter. Before I could take three steps to the door, the lights and sounds all came back on, and everything appeared normal except the ringing of a transmitter failure bell in the transmitter room. Instantly, I did a "To the rear march" and headed for the transmitters. The main TV transmitter was off, but it came back on when I pushed the reset button, and the alarm bell stopped ringing. I started the exhaust blower which had also tripped off, then checked the WHOM-FM transmitter which was all right. After checking all other equipment and assuring myself that normal operation had been restored, I returned to the living quarters. Something did not sound right at all. When I opened the switch room door I could hear a heavy pounding at 1200 beats per minute. The next door eight feet beyond the first leads directly into the engine room, and with that door open the sound was unbearable without the heavy ear protectors which we use for prolonged work in the engine room. It was obvious what had to be done. The other big engine, number two, had to be started and put on line, and number three, the one that was running and making all the noise had to be shut off. However, I was afraid that any moment number three engine might start throwing hot, jagged pieces of metal. I did not dare to go near it without someone else around who was aware of the problem. Dan, the night shift man, was still sleeping, so I pounded on his door and shouted, "We've got big trouble, I need help." Dan is a good mechanic, and as he woke up and heard the sounds coming from number three, It did not take him very long to realize the seriousness of the problem. In a few seconds he had his clothes on ready to go to work. I told Dan, "I'll go out and start number two, You just stand by in case number three blows up." I put on our best set of ear protectors, and climbed down the stairs to the engine room floor. It was like sneaking past an enemy machine gun site. It seemed to take forever to walk between the two big engines, open the sliding door into the plenum chamber, open the radiator slide in front of number two, come back between the engines, close the sliding door, then stand with that big, sick engine two feet from my back as I reached up to the controls on number two engine, turned the load limit control to 100%, Held the starter switch in the "glow plugs" position for a slow count to ten, then to start. As soon as it fired, I turned the governor knob thirteen half turns to full speed, then ran back to the switch room, where at least there wasn't so much physical danger. Quickly, I synchronized the generators and paralleled them, and as the circulating currents climbed rapidly, I jabbed the trip button on number three. Dan, watching through the doorway, said, "Oh no." Now at least we were powering the station with number two engine, but number three was still making just as much noise as it idled at full speed. To make matters worse, at about the time I tripped number three off the line, the side plates blew off and dumped seventy four gallons of hot oil and sixty gallons of hot antifreeze on the engine room floor. Dan and I agreed, "we've got to get that thing shut off somehow." Dan said, "You got number two started so I guess I'll try to get number three stopped." In order to avoid walking in the spilled oil and near the damaged part of the engine block, Dan had to climb over the generator, and reach past the air cleaners and the supercharger to reach the controls, but he was able to do it. Then, at last, we had peace and quiet with just the steady dull roar of number two smoothly powering the summit. Time for a quick cup of coffee and a bit of reflection before notifying John Ricker, Chief Engineer.

How we got into this mess is quite a story. When the station was built in 1954 the power plant consisted of three huge Caterpillar diesel electric generating sets. The "little" one was a D-8800, basically a D-7 bulldozer engine. The two main engines were D375s, huge V-8 engines weighing about 17,000 pounds each. They were 1662 cubic inches, eighteen to one compression ratio and supercharged with a gear driven Roots blower. Each engine required seventy four gallons of oil and sixteen oil filters, and sixty gallons of antifreeze mixture. They were slow turning engines, 1200 rpm, for extremely long life. With an oil change every couple of months and an overhaul every few years, these engines gave good reliable service. In 1981another D-375 became available for a reasonable price. It was most exactly the same age as our original two, but it had been an emergency plant at a hospital, and had run only a total of about six hundred hours, so channel eight bought it, and put it in the old Yankee powerhouse next door. There was quite a bit of discussion concerning what to do with it. Some of the possibilities were: Hook it up in the old Yankee powerhouse; put it in place of the little D-8800; use it for spare parts; wait until one of the old D375s was due for overhaul, then put this one in place of the old one. Opinions of expert diesel mechanics varied widely as to just what have we got. All the way from, "Six hundred hours total time, its practically a new engine. Switch it with one of the old ones and have something good that is going to last for many years." To, "As long as it has been sitting around not in use, gathering rust and age, you don't know, can't know what's inside. Don't trust it."

Finally, in the spring of 1983, it was decided that number three had run it's time long ago, and it should be overhauled or replaced this summer. Then it was decided to put the new/old engine in place of old number three. The company that was chosen to do the work will remain nameless because what happened subsequently was not entirely their fault. The work didn't actually get started until the end of August. It took only a few days to get one engine out of the building and the other one in and bolted down. Then as the hook up work started, it was found that there were more differences in the engines than had originally been supposed. The most obvious difference was that the new engine had been cooled with piped in cold water instead of a radiator. Once that set of problems had been dealt with, it was found necessary to switch the instruments and controls to the other side of the engine. Something no one had noticed before it was set in place. With all that corrected, it ran fine except that no oil was going to the external filter system. After quite a bit of head scratching it was found that the oil pump lacked the scavenge pump which is necessary for our hook up. With all the apparent problems solved, the next three months was a continuous story of leaks, squeaks, knocks, broken tubes and lines, overheats, unexplained slowdowns, shutdowns and governor irregularities. The engine would only run for a few days at a time, just long enough for a new problem to appear. Finally, on December 31 it was put on line and ran continuously until January 25 when it developed the loud pounding.

With all this in mind, it is easy to understand why chief engineer John Ricker was not too upset when I called him and told him, "Engine number three just blew up." After I told him all about it, he asked me if I could take the side plate the rest of the way off and see what I could see inside. By now the oil and antifreeze had drained down somewhat so a couple of bags of oil drying powder made a trail to the side of the now defunct engine. Much to my surprise, the side plate did not have any sharp dings in it, but was bulged and sprung as though from fluid pressure. Some bolts were sheared, others had pulled out and were laying against the side of number two engine, right where I had been standing as I started it. The few remaining bolts came out easily, and we were soon able to see inside. There were a few jagged pieces of broken piston laying in the bottom of the crankcase, and one connecting rod was not hitched to anything at the top end. The connecting rod, which weighs about forty pounds and is about eighteen inches long was still properly attached to the crankshaft. After the piston broke apart, the rod had been pounding in the cylinder at the full 1200 rpm until it broke a hole in the cylinder wall. This dumped the antifreeze mixture into the crankcase and is what blew the side plate off. After reporting all this to John Ricker, we were able to make our shift change. Two days later the diesel mechanics came up and officially pronounced the number three engine, "Junk."

This left us in a real mess, with just one main engine in the middle of winter. Number one engine, the old D-8800 is just not powerful enough to pull the summit load even with TV signed off. Some high management level decisions had to be made, and fast. A Caterpillar 3408 complete package power unit was obtained, and ways to transport it to the summit were explored. Due to its weight, a helicopter lift would have been way to expensive. Phil Labbie came back from retirement to supervise the move. While we made preparations on the Mountain to receive the new engine, Phil built a toboggan out of half inch steel plate and four inch angle iron. Paul Clark smoothed out and widened the road as best he could with our Thiokol Spryte snow tractor, and a D-6 bulldozer and driver were hired for the move. Eight days after the big blow up, everything was ready and the weather was right. It took five hours to travel the eight miles to the summit. Before dark, the engine was in the old Yankee power house. Two days later it was hooked up and able to pull the load. It was a strange sensation to have all the engines in the TV engine room shut off as we powered the summit from the new engine in the old Yankee power house. We soon found that we could do this only on comparatively mild days. On cold windy days, no amount of electric heat and kerosene salamanders could keep our building warm with no engine running in the engine room. At last, this brought the immediate crisis under control so that we could survive the winter and figure out our next move.

As the facts sifted down, it was found that a complete brand new package power unit, complete with engine, radiator, generator, controls and mounting frame, would cost less than an overhaul on one of the old V-8's. The new one would be more powerful, and a lot more efficient. Also, parts were getting hard to find for the long out of production D-375. Because number two had also run it's time a long time ago and was long overdue for overhaul, the decision was made to buy two new D-3406 complete units and put then in place of the old D-375's. To facilitate doing the change in an orderly fashion, we leased a 3306 in an outdoor housing and set that up outside the old Yankee powerhouse with wires running in the doorway to tie into the system. The plan was that at no time would we have less than two engines hooked up to pull the load. In summer weather we were able to clean everything except the old D-8800 out of the TV engine room and do a neat, workmanlike job of installing the new engines.

September 24, 1984, just eight months after the big blow up, the new engines were on line. Of course, there were still a few minor bugs to be worked out, but the new engines have proved to be one of the smartest things that WMTW-TV ever did.

The decision was made to buy the 3306 rental unit all except it's outdoor housing, to use for an emergency plant at the new studio in Auburn, Maine, not yet built. The 3408 was returned. The 3306 was then put in it's place inside the old Yankee powerhouse, where it was hooked up to serve as an extra engine here through the first winter with the new engines. In the spring of 1985, it was taken down the Mountain and installed in the new studio where it is just the right size to serve for emergency power.

We settled into a definite maintenance schedule with the new engines in that we would overhaul each one once, then trade it in the next time it was due for overhaul. One engine went bad in the winter when it was due for trade in the next summer, so we had to have it overhauled. Now that led to some head scratching. We really did not want to depend on it for another few years as a primary engine, but with a fresh overhaul it was too good to trade in. The answer was, we sold the old D-8800 which was too small for our load anyway, and put the overhauled engine in the old Yankee powerhouse next door, where it would be used only as a standby and emergency power plant. Now this was a really good arrangement because for the first time since the station began, we had the ability to run the engine in another building and have it quiet in the main engine room when we needed to do work there.

Later we got rid of the old, manually operated switch gear and replaced it with up to date equipment which would at the touch of a button start an engine, parallel it, switch it on line and share the load, then at the touch of another button take the other engine off load, switch it off line, and shut it down after a cool down period. If the engine on line started to get into trouble, such as an overheat, the system would automatically put another engine on line without even a flicker in the lights. If an engine quit with no warning, we would be dark for only about eight seconds. It was some kind of a trick to tear out the old switch gear, renovate the switch room, install the new stuff, and keep power on while we did it. Due to very careful planning by Dick Cushman, we were able to do it with just two planned and scheduled outages of about two hours each in the middle of the night to cause as few problems to as few people as possible. The new switch gear does have the capability of manual switching, or overriding the automatic features, but we never had to do that.

With the automatic switch gear and three good engines, when one is down for maintenance, we still have a spare in case the one we are running on should get into trouble. Also, we were able to do a much better job of keeping the engine room clean and workmanlike.

THE NEW WMOU-FM TOWER

At various times in 1987 we heard rumors that radio station WMOU in Berlin wanted to relocate their transmitter to the summit of Mount Washington. Steve Powell, the owner, had entered into a contract with WMTW-TV that we would provide space for a transmitter room and an antenna, but nothing much else seemed to be happening. We had also heard that the new owners of the Cog Railroad wanted to run a power line up the Mountain. Mr. Powell did not want to buy power from us, and therefore was interested in the Cog Railroad proposal. From time to time various people with impressive titles would show up on the summit, look around, ask questions, then go back to their offices to write reports. We saw some of these reports, and all of us mountain people agreed that everyone involved seemed to be greatly underestimating the cost, time and difficulties of such an undertaking and overestimating the benefits and the reliability. The power line idea died a natural death sometime in the summer of 1988.

The first real indication that something might really happen, was March 7, 1988, when Steve Powell called to tell us that he had received a construction permit from the FCC.

One of the hard learned lessons of Mount Washington is that most of the time outside work is very difficult due to the extreme weather conditions. The Auto Road is usually open to wheeled vehicles only from the middle of May to mid October. In June,

July and August, it is not reasonable to expect more than an average of two days a week when it is not raining in thick fog and high winds. Work crews have to spend a lot of time just waiting for a break in the weather, then have to move quickly when they can. By the first of September, the best days are none too good, and by the end of October, nothing except emergency repairs should be attempted. The message we mountain people try to get others to understand is this. If you plan to do outside construction work on the Mountain, have your plans all set and materials on hand when the road opens on Memorial Day. Any day that the clouds clear and the wind drops, get a big crew up here and work desperately hard until dark, even if it is on a week end or a holiday, and don't expect that it will be possible to work the next day. If you do get a few days in a row of good weather, take advantage of them all. If you have a ten day project that hasn't been started by the end of August, forget it until next year. This all sounds so much like exaggeration that no one will believe it until they have made all the same mistakes that we have seen so many times before.

With all this in mind, when we heard about the construction permit early in March, we thought that if Mr. Powell gets his act together quickly enough, gets orders in for tower, antenna, transmission line, transmitter and everything else, and gets a tower construction crew under contract, there may be hope for the station going on the air this year. Little did we realize that this project would turn into the most spectacular flail that we have ever seen.

Plans began to take shape. The transmitter room was easy. There is an addition to the north end of

Yankee Building which was originally a walk in cold storage room. For a number of years it had been used as a garage to store the Bombarder Muskeg tractor. Then later it was an annex to the Observatory's museum. Currently it was being used only to store lumber and odds and ends. On days when outside work was impractical, our summer work crew cleaned out this room and fixed it up. WMTW-TV Chief Engineer, Dick Cushman became the Contract Engineer for the construction. He did a very neat job of installing the new transmitters and all the things that go with them. That part was easy, the big problem was where and how to mount the antenna. A couple of quickly discarded ideas were to tear down the old Alford tower and put a new one in its place with the WMOU-FM antenna and a new WMTW-TV standby antenna, and/or get involved in some sort of joint effort with WHOM-FM for a shared antenna. Both of these ideas were soon rejected. Obviously, what would have to be done was to build some sort of a tower out back of Yankee building. Everyone in Channel 8 agreed that the new tower should be at least as far away from the building as it is high. Partly in case it falls down, it can't hit the building, but mostly to protect the building from falling ice. We didn't quite hold the line on that, however. As the facts sifted down, it was decided that the tower would be one hundred thirty feet tall, one hundred feet from the building. It would be a self supporting tower, that is, it would not have guy wires. It would be three legged, sixteen feet apart at the base, tapering to five feet at the seventy foot level, then five feet on a side the rest of the way, with a side mounted antenna. The base would be eighty tons of concrete. At that last remark, everyone on the Mountain began to worry. We were all very well aware that it is a matter of simple arithmetic that eighty tons of concrete is nowhere near enough to hold a tower of that size in very much wind, not to mention the ice load it would have to hold. We hoped that there was more to it than we had been told about, and a few weeks later we found out that there was. What really holds the tower is anchor bolts, twelve at each corner, over twenty feet long, over two inches diameter, set into bedrock, and tested to one hundred thousand pounds pull each. The only questions remaining were, could true bedrock be found at that location, and would the tower itself be strong enough? The more immediate problem was that calendar pages were turning, and nothing was happening except for the work inside the transmitter room. By the end of July, we were saying, "It can't happen this year, not enough good weather left." Finally, near the end of August, a Mr. John Corbin from Ellis Tower Company, Florida, showed up. He was about sixty years old, and the kind of a person who gets things done without a lot of unnecessary fooling around. His job was to put in the concrete base and the anchor bolts. The first thing he did was to make arrangement to get a road built around the end of Yankee building so that he could get equipment to the tower location. The second thing he did was to order a core drill so that he could find out what kind of rocks he had underneath the site to anchor to. After talking to Mr. Corbin I felt a lot better about the whole thing. At least, he knew the difference between boulders and bedrock, and what to do about it. If anything got done this fall, at least the base would be adequate. Mr. Powell talked to the core drilling company and told them that there was a good road to the site, they didn't need a track mounted drill, they could use a truck mounted drill. When the drill crew arrived with their truck mounted drill rig, they found that the road wasn't yet ready, and wouldn't be until the next day. So Mr. Powell had to pay for a day of waiting time. He admitted that it was his fault. This was one of the milder of many lessons he had to learn. Once the core drill was able to operate, real bedrock was found only seven feet down much to everyone's surprise and pleasure. Now serious work could begin, except that it was now the first of September. Mr. Corbin soon learned about another problem of Mountain work. The Auto Road management won't allow large trucks to come up or down the road except at night when the road is closed to the public, so it is necessary to plan carefully to get needed equipment up the Mountain no later than the night before it is needed. Also, many subcontractors charge a lot more for working at night or on week ends. With the problems of weather, transportation and scheduling, the tower base was finished and all the anchor rods installed October third. The tower was delivered to the base of the Auto Road on September 26. What an impressive collection of iron mongrey. The bottom leg sections are solid steel, not hollow pipe, but solid, twenty three inches in circumference, and all the other parts are proportionately as massive. The flanges where leg sections bolt together are three inches thick. At this point it appeared that maybe the tower would be adequate for Mount Washington conditions.

During this week, Dick Burwell, our summer laborer got through for the season, and Bob Walker, our perfectionist mechanical maintenance man changed to his winter duties, which means that instead of staying on the Mountain four days and three nights each week, he would work four, ten hour days at the studio. This was probably just as well. One of Bob's less popular duties had earned him the title of "Resident Bastard," which he was proud of. He had to "ride heard" on our customer's work crews to prevent them from stealing our tools and materials, and mounting antennas and feed lines in places we didn't want them to, and generally wrecking our buildings. If he had been on the summit with the tower crew, either they would have killed each other, or Bob would have been taken down in a straight jacket, or the tower crew would have staged a walk out strike. The thing to remember is that it was normal operation for Bob and the summer laborer to get through at this time because from now on there is just not enough good weather to do outside work.

On October seventh, we heard that the tower crew had been fired. This was not Ellis Tower Company which had put in the base, it was a different company. As we got the story, when Mr. Corbin left, he told Steve Powell that if the other company didn't work out, probably Ellis Tower Company could finish the job. When Dick Cushman and Steve Powell recognized that the other company had too many jobs going and wasn't taking this one seriously, the decision was made to change.

On October twelfth, A Mr. Bill Ellis the son of the owner of Ellis Tower Company, arrived to boss the job. His first time up the Mountain, and he had to be transported by our snow tractor from timberline up. Just a comedy side light to show how bad the weather was getting. On October eighth. The cog railroad had a locomotive run low on water on the summit, so they dumped the fire, drained the boiler and left it. It froze up, and it was two weeks before they could get it off the Mountain. The next two and a half months were the grandest fouled up mess that I have ever seen, and I have seen some dandies. Anywhere else, this tower job could have been done in less than a week. Here, if it could have been started in July instead of mid October, Three weeks at most. The first problem was for a bunch of Florida people to learn about cold weather operations. They had to obtain all sorts of cold weather clothing, and learn about working on an ice covered tower. It took a while for them to realize that the best weather they would get would be worse than the kind that anywhere else would cause them to take the day off. From time to time we were able to get the road open to wheeled vehicles long enough to get various pieces of heavy equipment up or down. Paul Clark, our snow tractor driver had to make many trips with our vehicles transporting people and tools. All the pieces of the tower were brought up, together with a portable winch, and a truck mounted crane called a Stinger, and a tool truck. The tower crew turned out to be, to put it as politely as possible, an interesting bunch to have around. It is difficult to believe that anyone could make so much mess so quickly. They soon learned that things left outdoors would soon get covered with snow. When they stayed in Yankee building, we had to feed them which was a lot of extra work for us. We received and had to deal with many 'phone calls some business related, but many from wives and/or girl friends. One problem was that they should have had a job foreman on the Mountain and an expediter in the valley to hunt up equipment and such. Bill Ellis tried to do both jobs himself, so he frequently wasn't where he was needed most. By now the summit was littered with tools, equipment and tower parts all mixed with the snow, and there was plywood from an unsuccessful attempt at building some sort of a shelter for some of their equipment.

November first found them with the bottom seventy feet of the tower completed except for some of the cross bracing. Mr. Ellis was not on the Mountain, and a storm was moving in. The crew on the Mountain panicked, decided to leave, and take the Stinger crane down with them so it would not get wintered in. No one is exactly sure what happened, or at least no one would admit to it, but they soon had the Stinger crane stuck crosswise between the rocks on the service road about one hundred feet below the summit on a 31% grade, with a broken drive shaft and locked brakes. On the shift change the next day we had to walk up from the lower parking lot because the Stinger crane was blocking the road. Later, Paul built a road around it out of packed snow. Needless to say, when Mr. Ellis found out about it he was somewhat wilder than he usually was. In his defense, it should be pointed out that a less gung ho person could not have built that tower under those conditions. Anyone of milder temperament would have said "To heck with this foolishness, I'll see you in the spring." He was the right person in the right place at the right time. When presented with seemingly insurmountable problems, he would get a wild look in his eyes and say " I AM going to build that tower."

Getting the Stinger unstuck was the first order of

business. It was necessary to pay a truck mechanic $250 per day in addition to his regular overtime pay just to come up the Mountain. Two timber skidders were hired also. One skidder was able to winch the Stinger down into the lower parking lot so that the mechanic could work on it. Portable kerosene heaters called salamanders and a small gasoline electric generator were brought up to thaw out equipment. After the Stinger was repaired, Bill Ellis drove it back up to the summit blowing the air horn all the way, he was so excited. After he parked it, he was literally jumping with joy and letting out all sorts of rebel yells.

Now some hard decisions had to be made. After much figuring, head scratching and telephone calls, it was decided that there was only one way the tower could be put up this winter. All the pieces of the top sections of the tower were loaded onto trailers and hauled back down the road by skidders to be assembled in the field by the toll house at the base, then brought back and set in place by helicopter. This idea was not as far out as it sounds, because there was a Skycrane building a power line over on the New Hampshire/Vermont border, only about a half hour flying time away. There was just one little detail wrong with this plan. We never did get weather that was quite good enough for the Skycrane to do it's stuff. The Skycrane left for another job in Alaska on December third. That required some drastic rethinking. The top sixty feet of the tower was now assembled in the Glen House field near the toll gate. The one thing we did have going for us was that so far there wasn't a lot of snow. It was still possible with a lot of plowing with our snow tractors to get the road open to large wheeled vehicles such as skidders. It was still on the fringes of possibility to bring a large truck mounted crane up the road, if nothing else went wrong. Ellis's Stinger was nowhere near big enough. Dan Taillon of Gorham had several large cranes including at least one that would be adequate for the job. Dan had done crane work on the summit in the summer season and didn't think much of the idea, but Mr. Powell offered him so much money that he couldn't refuse. Bringing a huge crane like that up the Mountain in the winter is not just a matter of fill the fuel tank and go. Special custom built tire chains had to be made for all wheels of which there are twelve, tandem in front and dual tandem in rear. Two hundred gallons of special thin winter weight hydraulic oil had to be obtained to replace the standard hydraulic oil in the system. Some of the fenders and mudguards had to be removed to make room for the tire chains. The tower sections were loaded onto flatbed trailers after special cradles were built, then hauled up the road with skidders. Then it was just a matter of waiting for the brief and infrequent breaks in the weather which would allow anything to be done. For example, it quickly became apparent that the crane did not have power enough to swing a tower section against a wind greater than about fifty mph, and the wind seldom dropped below fifty. Mostly, we just sat around and got on each others nerves. Some of the events of one Wednesday morning show the way things were going. We were out of bacon and eggs so I served the crew creamed chipped beef on toast. As closely as I can remember it, here are the words of Bill Ellis's after breakfast speech "If Dan Taillon doesn't quit stalling around, I'll take my chain saw with the metal cutting blade and kill him and cut his crane up in little pieces and throw it over the edge, and then we're going to buy a gas grill and a case of eggs and a side of beef and a lot of other things and we're going to do our own cooking in Yankee building, and we'll get a case of duct tape to tie and gag that stupid Art Dunlap, tie him to one of the machines so he can't be bothering my men!" About an hour later the other shift arrived for the shift change. Just as they walked through the door, I had just finished washing and putting away the dishes, some of which were left over from the night before. Art Dunlap started to chew me out about not shoveling the snow in front of the door. There was a drift that wasn't more than six inches deep to begin with, and there had ten men including myself in and out several times that morning so the snow was pretty well tramped down and kicked out of the way. Ordinarily, I don't get too excited about things like that, but with the other problems we had going, Art's remark about shoveling snow was so far out of touch with reality that something snapped. I yelled at him, "look, the good news is that the building is still standing, anything else you just have to take it as you find it!" I think I said quite a few more things too, before I calmed down.

The rest is an anticlimax. The next day the last major piece of the tower was in place. As soon as the hoist line was unhooked Dan had the boom coming down and the outriggers coming up. I think he started to roll almost before everything was stowed, he was in such a rush to get down. The tower crew finished the details and hung the antenna and feed line, and three weeks later left for Florida. The station went on the air on New Years Day with only a few more details to be completed on the tower in the spring.

The station has been sold several times and is now WPKQ. After a rather lumpy beginning it has operated quite well with only the expected amount of problems.

A New TV Transmitter

Off the air! Panic! The main TV transmitter was being worked on, and now the standby had quit. It took twenty minutes to put the main rig back together, warm it up and put it on the air. Twenty minutes with no channel eight in the three state region. This was in February of 1997. It happened on the other shift so I didn't hear the details until I came to work on Wednesday. The problem was simple enough. The special motor controlled buck/boost filament regulator transformer for the visual ten kilowatt tube had burned up. No replacement was available, so our boss, Dick Cushman, bypassed it to make the rig useable in an emergency, although we could never again depend on it. Large, high power transmitting tubes cost thousands of dollars and are very sensitive to filament voltage. With no filament regulator the rig would work very well, but not for very long.

We had been off the air for twenty minutes. In TV broadcasting, air time is precious. Figuratively speaking, they smelled the smoke all the way out to the corporate offices in Pennsylvania. Of course, their first reaction was to chew out Dick for it. His reply was, "this is what I have been trying to tell you for years. The standby transmitter is the one we started with in 1954, it is forty three years old, and has 175,000 hours of operating time on it. Insulation is dried out, lots of things in it are weak, worn out or burned up from old age, and replacement parts are mostly unavailable. If you think that we have a reliable standby transmitter, you are kidding yourselves. Also, the main transmitter is sixteen years old, has over 130,000 hours on it and the company that made it is out of business. You know how much trouble we have had with it for years. We need a new transmitter." The powers that be at corporate saw the light, or perhaps I should say they saw the darkness of potential lost air time. Their reaction changed from, "No way" to, "We've got to have a new transmitter right now, how soon can you get it?" Fortunately Dick had been studying the problem for a long time. He knew what was needed, what was available, and how to specify it for ordering. Ordinarily it takes six months to a year to get this sort of equipment because the factory doesn't start to make it until they have an order. Apparently Paul Harron, owner of the parent corporation of channel eight, must have some pull in the industry because we were able to get moved ahead on a production list to get delivery in a couple of months. Unfortunately we had a couple of other things going. The summer before, we had a new roof put on our building. For unknown reasons, part of it blew off, and every warm day we had water leaking everywhere. All we could do was mop and bail until we could get the roofing crew up in the middle of the winter to do some emergency patching to try to hold back the water until summer when it could be fixed right. The other problem was one which we had been thinking about for many years and had started on before the roof problem and the transmitter problem appeared. The plan was to completely rearrange all of the small electronic equipment, install new racks to mount it in, and rewire everything. This included the microwave receivers and transmitters with their power supplies and subcarrier units, and all the control, monitoring, switching, communications, alarms, and video and audio processing equipment. Obviously it is some kind of a trick to do this without interrupting the TV programming. Also included in the plan was to build a wall to make a room for the small rack mounted equipment separate from the transmitter room. Part of this was to build a new workbench area inside the new room, and a bookcase and cabinet which included space for the fax machine, computer printer and the copy machine. All in all a major project in itself, and we were far enough along with it that we had to continue with it.

As soon as a firm order had been placed with Harris Radio Corporation, they loaned us a two kilowatt transmitter to be used as a standby while we tore out the old one and installed the new one. The loaner turned out to be just two units. The transmitter itself was about the size of a refrigerator, and the diplexer which combines the visual and aural output to go to the antenna was about the size of a two drawer file cabinet. We already had an excellent main/standby switch in the transmission line to the antenna, so it was no big deal to disconnect the output from the old transmitter and connect the output from the loaner. A cable for a.c. from a thirty amp breaker, and audio and video feeds from the confused mess that was now our control equipment, and we had a low power but good standby. No warm up or cool down, just on and off. We tried it on the air and Jack Conner, Chief Engineer at the studio, had trouble believing that it was only two kilowatt. Before disconnecting the output line from the old rig, we did run it one last time, and I had the honor of shutting off the switch for the last time. After which I wrote in the log "Well done good and faithful servant."

Now came the hard part, taking apart and getting rid of the old rig. It was a 1954 RCA TT-10/25BH television transmitter. According to the instruction manuals the parts we had to get rid of weighed about 17,500 pounds. The main part of the rig consisted of eight cabinets seven feet high and three feet deep bolted together forming a line twenty four feet long. Behind that was three high voltage transformers each about the size of a chest type deep freezer, and another cabinet which housed the output tubes for the 25 kilowatt visual amplifier. On the back wall and on the ceiling there was another four thousand pounds of RF plumbing and large tank like cavities, things with names like notch diplexer, harmonic filter and vestigial sideband filter. The plan was to first do a quick hit and run job of picking off anything that looked like it might be worth saving. This yielded surprisingly little stuff. Then not very gently we disassembled things to pieces small enough for two men to lift to carry out into the parking lot and throw onto a pile. Some of the heavy stuff overhead required some careful work with ropes, pulleys and comealongs to get it down safely. The high voltage transformers weighed about 1100 pounds each, so we moved them over to the door with crowbars and pipe rollers, then hooked a chain onto then and used the snow tractor to yard them out and push them onto the pile. Of course the first thing we had done was to shut off and remove the wires that supplied electrical power to the rig, but even so, as we worked we would have a flash of sparks and take a nick out of a wire cutter or other tool as we found a wire that still had electricity on it. Each one required a lot of wondering and tracing wires to find out where it came from and how to shut it off without shutting off something which we were still using. Although the rig had uncountable thousands of man hours spent on it over the years cleaning, troubleshooting and preventative maintenance, we found many parts deep within it which as we looked at them we had to say, "Now how could that have still been working?" Many electrical connections fell apart when touched. At one point we found what we thought was an insulating blanket of some sort, but then we realized that it was simply forty years accumulation of hard packed dust and dirt. After taking out cooling ductwork, electrical conduits and supporting iron mongery we had quite an impressive pile of scrap metal out in the parking lot. As we admired the pile, the joking remark was made, "For sale cheap, one slightly used TV transmitter, working when taken out of service, some reassembly required." What we took out was electrically three transmitters, a ten kilowatt aural, a ten kilowatt visual and a twenty five kilowatt visual amplifier and their associated combiners. Originally there had been a twenty five kilowatt aural amplifier, but that had been taken out in 1981 to make room for the RCA TTG-17H which was our main transmitter from then on.

The new Harris HT-20HS transmitter had been delivered to our garage in Gorham, and was sitting there in crates ready to be brought up the Mountain as soon as the road was open to wheeled vehicles. But another problem set in. This one worked in our favor however. In the month of may we received just under eight feet of snow in a series of storms. The Auto Road crew had a terrible time of it. It was the only time anyone can remember that they were not able to open to the public by Memorial Day. Several times they would open up a section of the road and park their equipment for the night. The next day we would use our snow tractor to bring them up to rescue their equipment and plow down to reopen what they had opened previously. This all worked in our favor however because it gave us time to do a very good job of laying a new floor and getting lots of things ready before we moved the new rig in. We thought it might take a week to get the new transmitter up and all summer to get rid of the junk pile. Dick rented a small but powerful van truck with a hydraulic elevator tail gate. When the auto road crew told us we could go, it took thirty six hours to get the new rig up, and two days to get the old one down. Admittedly, this was pushing it, but we were desperate to see the last of that scrap metal. Ten days later the new rig was on the air for it's first test run.

The old RCA TT-10/25BH was all vacuum tubes, everything in series, one stage driving the next. If anything went wrong at any point, the whole thing quit working. It made a lot of waste heat, which means that it used a lot more power than it actually put out as transmitter power. The big tubes required as much as five thousand volts. The heat and high voltage was constantly cooking parts and attracting dirt. Tubes age, requiring frequent adjustment, retuning and replacement. The big ones cost thousands of dollars each and the small ones are getting hard to find. It seems to be a characteristic of every big vacuum tube transmitter that I have worked with that every now and again when you are least expecting it, and for no apparent reason, the rig will shut down. Usually it will come back by itself, but sometimes it will stay off until the operator on duty pushes the reset button. All big transmitters have a variety of malfunction indicators which are quite informative when you have a real problem, but on these random trips you may get one or several, and it appears that some or all of them may be just a reaction to the sudden shut down. The suspicion is that it may be dust build up on an insulator has zapped across and cleaned itself, a piece of cathode material has flaked off and caused a momentary short, or an insect may have landed on an arc gap and been vaporized. Which leads to the remark, "That transmitter is the most expensive bug zapper in the North Country." Anyway, these short outages are irritating to the viewers, very irritating to the front office and they don't leave the transmitter crew very calm either.

The Harris HT-20HS is just three cabinets bolted together six feet high four feet deep and eight feet long, with a diplexer about four feet square out back and a few hundred pounds of RF plumbing and combiners overhead. It is all solid state, no tubes. Except for a little bit of low power stuff in the instrumentation and control cabinet, the highest voltage in it after the mains is only fifty volts. Most of the power it uses becomes transmitted RF power, so there is not a lot of waste heat. All the high power stages are essentially in parallel with plenty of reserve gain. If anything goes wrong, the rig keeps working at full power and a green light on the failed module turns red. The failed module can be pulled out and replaced with a spare or the rig can run without it while it is being sent back to the factory for repairs. There is no loss of output power and not even a flicker in the picture when a module is pulled out or replaced. It is generally understood that when a piece of equipment is brand new you can expect a few problems, and we did have a couple of minor failures.

After that it just runs and runs. It doesn't seem to have any nasty tricks that are an inherent part of it's design. Without excessive heat or high voltage, it doesn't sit there sucking up dirt. We have been able to completely overhaul the 1981 RCA TTG-17H to make it as good as a vacuum tube rig can be so we have a good standby transmitter which is hardly ever needed now.

An interesting sidelight on all this is that when the station was being built in 1954, it was a race against time to get it built before winter made outside work and heavy hauling impossible. While the building was being constructed on the Mountain, Chief Engineer, Parker Vincent and his crew assembled and tested the transmitter in a rented space in Manchester. Then they disassembled it, moved it to the Mountain and reassembled it. Including the twenty five kilowatt amplifier, it would have weighed about twenty two thousand pounds of equipment, most of which was quite delicate and had to be handled carefully. Considering how hard we worked just to get rid of it, it is amazing to consider how hard Parker and his crew worked to build it. At that time, commercial TV broadcasting was brand new. These were all experienced radio engineers, but this was probably the first TV transmitter any of them had ever seen, and certainly the biggest and most complicated rig that any of them had ever worked on. It worked well for twenty seven years and then served as a standby for sixteen more years.

THE LAST CHAPTER

The beginning of the end came with the widespread use of solid state electronics equipment which, once it was set up and adjusted, could run for months or years without further attention. In the days when vacuum tube equipment was the only way to go, broadcast stations and transmitters required constant monitoring, tinkering and adjustment by highly skilled, trained and motivated people who were referred to as Engineers, although in many cases their only formal certification was the FCC First Class Radiotelephone Operator License which was required to work on broadcast transmitters. It is the nature of vacuum tube equipment that as the tubes age and as other components deteriorate from the heat of the tubes, the operating parameters drift and require frequent adjustment to maintain performance to required standards. In the old days the station would sign off for a few hours every night, and we spent many hours testing tubes, replacing the weak or shorted ones, and cleaning out the dirt that was attracted by the heat and high voltage. As the years went by, we replaced one by one the old equipment with new units which almost never needed attention after installation. In most cases, when any of the new stuff fails, it cannot practically be repaired outside the factory. I tend to suspect that in most cases the factory does not attempt to troubleshoot in the old fashioned sense, they just throw the whole circuit board in the trash and put in a new one. In many cases if we could find the trouble and obtain replacement parts, the unit would require alignment which can only be done with lots of expensive equipment which we don't have. If anyone does repair something in the field, it is never right again. That was a big change from the days when we could fix anything with a few basic tools and test instruments.

After the solid state revolution, most broadcast stations remote controlled their transmitters and no longer had a crew on site. They just have someone from the studio come to the transmitter once in a while. Many stations just have a contract person who also takes care of several stations. The FCC gradually eased the requirements of what had to be done. Years ago, we had to read and log the transmitter meters every half hour, then it was every three hours, then it was not at all, although we continued to read the meters every six hours. The new rule is, do whatever is necessary to maintain legal operation. As a practical matter, modern transmitters can run for months or years without drifting outside of legal limits. So basically, stations can usually get away with ignoring everything until something fails completely. For a long while I realized that the job was going out from under me. Sometime about 1984, the FCC eliminated the requirement for the First Class license to work on broadcast transmitters. The justification for this was that the station is licensed, it is the responsibility of the licensee to see to it that the rules are adhered to. When we renewed our licenses we got lifetime non expiring General Class licenses which we were told replaced both the old First and Second Class. We in the industry felt that this made about as much sense as why not eliminate licenses for airline pilots, ship captains, truck drivers and medical doctors because airliners, ships, trucks and hospitals all are licensed, it is the responsibility of the licensee to see to it that the rules are adhered to. Another thing which I considered to be a low blow insult was when the company personnel directory was revised, our title was changed from "Transmitter Engineer" to "Transmitter Technician." Of course an insult doesn't hurt unless it is true, and in this case I realized that due to the changes in technology it was about right. The job which I had studied for, trained for and worked for all my life, no longer existed.

For many years the station management had wanted to remote control the transmitter on Mount Washington and eliminate our jobs. Some of the reasons why they couldn't do that was that up until 1997 the standby transmitter was the old 1954 TT-10/25BH which due to it's age was even less stable than it was in the days when half hour log readings were required, and the main transmitter installed in 1981 had never been as dependable as it should have been. Due to the remoteness of the site, at best it would take a couple of hours to get to, and at worst during winter storms, it could take several days. Also was the problem of taking care of the diesel electric generating plant and the tank farm and pipeline with a years supply of fuel. Then was the problem of regulating the intake of cooling air, to keep the equipment from either freezing or overheating and to avoid filling the place up with snow or melt water. The idea of remote control came up from time to time, but it never went very far due to one or more of the above reasons.

The real kick to do something different came with the federal mandate to build a digital TV station. For technical reasons it was not practical to do that on the Mountain, and it was felt that due to changes in

147

demographics (whatever that means) it would be better to broadcast from closer to Portland Maine. Also, it would be nice to be able to reach the site without a major arctic expedition. Some land was purchased in Baldwin Maine, and legal battles were fought and won. When all the paperwork was right, a road was built, then a cement building and a 1700 foot tall tower. Now here is where one idea leads to another, and another. Early in the planning it was decided that with a tower and a building close to Portland, it made sense to move the Channel 8 transmitter and have everything in one place, remote controlled and accessible. Another idea is interlocked into this. The digital transmitter had to be built for a UHF channel. For technical reasons, a VHF channel such as Channel 8 is much more desirable. One of the rules is that if and when analog NTSC TV is eliminated (in 2006 the FCC hopes) stations can keep whichever of the two channels they are now using. With up to date transmitters it is a simple overnight change to modify an analog transmitter to digital. This possibility was carefully considered with long term goals in mind in 1997 when a new transmitter was purchased for the Mountain.

The Harris transmitter we purchased is modular in nature. One cabinet houses the controls and exciter, then as many amplifier cabinets are used as are necessary to make the needed power. Each cabinet contains two power supplies and seventeen modules, On the Mountain we were assigned a lower power level because of the altitude which of course makes the signal go further. We needed two amplifier cabinets on the Mountain, but would need four at Baldwin, so the new transmitter was bought with the understanding that we would need two more cabinets later. The original idea was to get everything ready at Baldwin, then run on the 1981 RCA transmitter for the week or two that it would take to move the Harris transmitter and hook it up. Then we would shut off the RCA and turn on the Harris and that would be the end of TV from Mount Washington. At one point, the plan was to get all this done by November 1, 2001. The reason for picking that date was that it was about as late as we could count on getting a truck up the Mountain to transport the cabinets. Like everything in life, things took longer than expected, so a new date had to be picked, February 1, 2002, That meant that the move down the Mountain had to be done by snow tractor. This was no problem for the amplifier modules and power supplies, and all the other control and monitoring equipment that had to be moved. But the empty cabinets themselves which weigh about a thousand pounds each and are about the size and shape of a very large refrigerator, those would be a problem. The solution was that because we had a new control and exciter cabinet at Baldwin, that one didn't have to be moved in the winter. We were able to buy two more empty but wired amplifier cabinets so they wouldn't have to be moved. This was practical because the modules and power supplies were the expensive part. We also borrowed a one kilowatt transmitter from Harris Radio Company which we could hook up for a spare in case anything went wrong with the RCA transmitter while we were moving the new transmitter.

The final count down started January 20, 2002 when Dick Cushman, Paul Clark, and the Harris Radio crew came up the Mountain to convert the twenty kilowatt Harris transmitter into a ten kilowatt rig. They removed the combiner which coupled the two amplifier cabinets and took the amplifier modules and power supplies from one cabinet to Baldwin. We ran at half power for a week. Then Dick and Paul came up again to finish the job. We switched to the old 1981 RCA transmitter for it's final run. Then we hooked up the one kilowatt rig in place of the Harris transmitter and removed everything else from the Harris cabinets to go to Baldwin. Now we were thoroughly committed to have to get the Baldwin site going as quickly as possible. Of course, Murphey's law caught up with us. The next day the RCA transmitter developed problems which were not readily fixable so we could only run at about half power, but that was the same as we had with half the Harris transmitter, so it was ok, not good but ok.

Finally the big day arrived. Tuesday February 5, the TV transmitter on Mount Washington was turned off for the last time and the one at Baldwin was turned on. I was on my regular time off, so Dick called me at home to tell me. I never was able to receive channel eight very well at home because of a range of mountains about five miles away which mostly blocked the signal. It always was weak and ghosty. With a five element yagi antenna pointed at the Mountain the best that I could get was ninety microvolts of signal. Five hundred to a thousand is considered good. I have always picked up Channel 6 and 13 with a stacked batwing antenna which was made by my uncle, Roger Carlson of Carslon and Obard Antenna Company about fifty years ago. After the switch, I had one thousand microvolts on the yagi which of course was now pointing in the wrong direction, and three thousand microvolts on the antique batwing antenna. The picture looked as good as the ones on the Mountain direct out of the microwave equipment.

The NAB (National Association of Broadcasters) handbook states that anyone building a new station should expect that it should take about three years. In our case, from the time the first machine was unloaded at the base of the hill to build the road until the transmitter was put on the air for real was ten days less than a year.

Of course, until other arrangements could be made, we still had to have a crew on the Mountain to operate the diesel electric generating plant and other things. My sixty fifth birthday was April 28, 2002, so most any time would have been good enough for me to retire. The hard part was from early 2001 on, of not knowing what was going to happen and when.

Without the waste heat from the transmitter, and with the reduced load on the generators, for the rest of the winter it was moderately tricky to maintain heat in the building. The building never had much in the way of a heating system, depending on waste heat from the equipment. We had a few electric heaters in the living quarters but that was all. We put two 3.3 kilowatt heaters down cellar, and got a few portable, home type electric heaters to use in the transmitter room, and were able to stay reasonably comfortable through the rest of the winter.

Spring came, the snow melted and the road was opened for the summer. We had not really been looking forward to the job of moving out the Harris cabinets and the old RCA transmitter. It would have been quite a job for us. Early in June, Cotte Riggers was hired to move the big stuff, so that was quite a relief. We could handle all the small stuff easily enough ourselves, although it did take quite a few truck loads. The plan was to sell the Mountain operation to the State of New Hampshire. They would add it to their Mount Washington State Park, and they needed our generators anyway. That was a whole lot easier said than done, and with a whole State Capitol full of lawyers to argue about it, there was no telling how long it would take. WMTW company management notified the customers who we supplied power to and who had radio equipment in our buildings that we would no longer be servicing them after June 30. None of us had any idea what that would mean. Personally, my sixty fifth birthday had passed, so I had planned to retire at about that time anyway, but I told my boss that I would stick around as long as he needed me. When I came to work Wednesday, June 26, Dick told me to pack up to send to Baldwin all the rest of the stuff in the electronics work bench cabinets. I did that and made the comment that when that stuff left, we were completely out of the electronics business. We were down to slim pickings for things to do and things to work with. Dick came up Friday morning to take the stuff down, then Friday afternoon, Jack Connor, Chief Engineer, called and set up a conference call with Dave Kaufman, Station Manager and company Vice President, who told us that everything was all set and the State would take over at ten a.m. Sunday. All that last week, every chore that I did, I thought, "This may be the last time I do that." After Jack and Dave's call, I thought, "This is the last time I do that." Don Gauthier and I packed up the last of our stuff and did the usual shift change clean up. It just happened to work out that my license was the last one to come down off the wall. Saturday night/Sunday morning I really did not sleep very well in expectation of finally getting off the Mountain for the last time. When Dick came up Sunday morning to take us down, it did not take long to load our stuff, turn in our keys, sign off the logs for the last time and head down. We reached the base about nine a.m., said our goodbys and went our separate ways.

As I drove, I left the broadcast receiver turned off, as it seemed like a time for deep thinking. The Amateur radio was on however. In Maine, there is an elaborate, good working system of linked repeaters, the creation of one man, Dave Hawke KQ1L. The Twelve County Emergency Net meets there on Sunday morning, and I usually check in on my way to church. This morning it came on as I was starting up Evens Notch. I checked in and it was fun to report that I was retired, "As of about a half hour ago." After I got home, unloaded the car and had some lunch, my wife and I went to the flea market at Fryeburg Fair Grounds. It was lots of fun to talk to people and tell them, "I am now retired as of about four hours ago."

I never set out to be a TV personality, but I just went with the flow and took what came. The way things worked out. I had just enough fame and recognition to be fun but not a burden. For me, the job ended just about when I was going to retire anyway. There can be no regrets or looking back because the job which was a major part of my life for so many years no longer exists.

As for my coworkers, Dick Cushman was still Assistant Chief Engineer for Channel 8 and also has a part time job with the State managing the generating plant. "Drew," Andrew Knightly already had a job with Yankee Microwave. Peter Cushman had always thought of the job as temporary anyway as he wanted to go back to college. Paul Clark, our mechanic and tractor driver, was only out of work about three hours. The State hired him for just about exactly the same job. The only one who was really out of work was Don Gauthier, and last time I talked to him, he wasn't worried about it, he figured that he could find something.

Now I am enjoying my retirement. I can start on a project without being under the pressure of having to leave it for a week. No longer am I faced with the problem that any kind of a club meeting or anything that happened on a particular day of the month, I would go in and out of phase with it on a three month cycle. For this reason, there were many things which I could never get deeply into while I was working. I still watch Channel 8 news and a few things on Channel 10, but that's about it. After watching TV two or more monitors at a time for sixteen hours a day seven days a week, one week out of two for thirty eight years, I am just not that interested in watching TV.

EPILOGUE

Sunday, February 9, 2003: It was a nice day, so my wife and I decided to go to Norway/ South Paris. On the way home, about 5:00 p.m. I heard someone on the Amateur two meter radio ask someone else if he had any idea what was happening on Mount Washington. He said that he had heard a news item about a fire or something on the Mountain, and also WHOM-FM was off the air. The other person didn't know anything about it, and I didn't either, so I stayed silent. We were almost home, so after I parked in the barn, before I left the car, I tuned the broadcast receiver to WHOM-FM. Nothing. Then I tuned to WPKQ-FM. Nothing there either. WPKQ-FM is in another building, so the power must be off. I considered calling Dick Cushman, but decided against it as he probably was up to his neck in problems as it was. On the Channel 6 news, there was a brief item about it, saying there had been a fire, but it didn't say much else. About 6:45 p.m. Dick called me to tell me that as we speak, the entryway was burning, the rest of the building was gone. He said the Observatory crew reported finding the engine room full of smoke. He asked them if it was high or low, and they said, "High." Dick thought, "That's where the diesel exhausts go through the wall." He asked them to look outside. They reported that the whole wall was aflame. In a seventy five mph wind there was no hope of fighting it, so he said, "Don't try to be a hero, just get out of there," which they did. Dick sent Paul up with the Piston Bully snow tractor to take the crew down. The fire also destroyed the Old Yankee Powerhouse, so all three generators were gone in addition to the switch gear. Also gone was the distribution panels and the fuel distribution valves, so the summit was in the most desperate situation it had ever been in.

The next day the Observatory crew came back with a couple of small portable generators, then a few days later two 30 kilowatt generators. The most urgent thing was to get fuel to the generators and furnaces. That was done, then gradually the summit returned to normal operation so far as radios and heat was concerned.

Now, as this book goes to press, the summit is littered with generators, fuel lines, wires, cables, waveguides, etc. Deep thinking is being done as to, "Where do we go from here?" Lots of ideas are being explored, the power line from the base is a strong possibility. One thing is for sure however, never again will full time resident Engineers be a part of it.

The era is past. The big rigs no longer require the constant loving attention of dedicated resident engineers. It is no longer desirable for the antenna to be the highest point in eight hundred miles. The transmitters are now moved to an obscure hill twenty five miles from Portland. The building no longer stands, and no longer do mountain men proudly hang their licenses on the wall and call themselves engineers.

Order Form

Martin Engstrom
227 West Fryeburg Road
Fryeburg, ME 04037

Please send: Marty on the Mountain

Price: $16.95 Each

Shipping: $ 3.00 Each

Sales Tax: $ 0.85 Each
(For books shipped to Maine Address)

Qty._____Amount Enclosed $_____

Name_____

Address_____

City _____

State _____ Zip Code _____

This page may be photocopied.